D1497949

.3

a

1 vocab
2 Eng — — gloss, vocab
                        etc

-l

Building Your Vocabulary

BUILDING YOUR VOCABULARY

by

JOHN G. GILMARTIN, Litt.D.

Superintendent of Schools, Waterbury, Connecticut

*Author of "Word Study," "Everyday Errors in
Pronunciation," and others.*

WITH REVISIONS

LIBRARY
LUTHERAN BIBLE INSTITUTE
IN CALIFORNIA
641 S. WESTERN AVENUE
ANAHEIM, CA 92804

1963

PRENTICE-HALL, INC.

Englewood Cliffs, N. J.

PE
1449
.G47
1963

COPYRIGHT, 1939, 1950, BY

PRENTICE-HALL, INC.

ALL RIGHTS RESERVED. NO PART OF THIS BOOK
MAY BE REPRODUCED IN ANY FORM, BY MIMEO-
GRAPH OR ANY OTHER MEANS, WITHOUT PER-
MISSION IN WRITING FROM THE PUBLISHERS.

PRINTED IN THE UNITED STATES OF AMERICA

08916—E

Preface

Every person who wishes to succeed in life should develop the ability to express himself fluently and accurately. This skill may be perfected only through the acquisition of a large vocabulary. One need only note the number of people among his own acquaintances who occupy responsible positions and, although they never attended college, have a strong command of English, to illustrate the practical advantage of an effective vocabulary. The ease and precision of expression possessed by the leaders of various businesses and professions are familiar to everyone. A large vocabulary is an important element in success.

Vocabulary building is a subject of universal interest, and it is a field that is open to anyone who desires to speak well. Some subjects may never be thoroughly mastered by some students, even with intensive study. But anyone who will devote a small amount of effort for the purpose may acquire a forceful and enviable vocabulary in a short time.

The purpose of this book is to present to the reader the shortest and surest way to effect a worthwhile vocabulary. Many people think that the possession of a large vocabulary means the ability to clothe one's thoughts in words of unusual length. Actually, it is the direct opposite. The man who takes five words to do the work of one has the wrong kind of vocabulary. An adequate vocabulary enables one to express his thoughts succinctly.

The lessons in this book are diversified. Some contain words that you recognize but do not use. Some are devoted to common words that are mispronounced by the great majority. To add these to your store of useful words, incorporate them in sentences, and then pronounce them aloud. Try them out on objects—animate or inanimate. Hearing yourself say these words will have the salutary effect that using them in conversation has, and will prepare the way for actual use.

Some lessons are devoted to words frequently confused. In building your vocabulary, you must not concentrate on new words and neglect to check yourself on old words that you have not yet mastered.

If the reader will devote a reasonable amount of time to the reading, practice, and self-checks in this book, he will soon sense the gradual disappearance of self-consciousness and timidity in speaking, and the emergence of self-assurance and confidence.

Quoted definitions in this book are reprinted from: (1) *Webster's New International Dictionary,* Second Edition, Copyright, 1934, by G. & C. Merriam Company, Springfield, Mass.; (2) *The Standard Dictionary,* copyrighted by Funk & Wagnalls Company, New York, N. Y.; and (3) *The Winston Simplified Dictionary,* Advanced Edition, copyrighted by The John C. Winston Company, Philadelphia, Pa., with the permissions of the publishers.

J. G. G.

Contents

*171 VOCABULARY BUILDERS

viii   Contents

Contents

Gilmartin's Sixty Snags in Pronunciation

The pronunciations recorded in this book conform with those found in Merriam-Webster, Winston, Thorndike, and New Standard dictionaries. *February, 1949.*

Gilmartin's Sixty Snags in Pronunciation

That people desire to increase their vocabulary cannot be denied, and that they are just as zealous but more sensitive about their pronunciation seems to be the general fact. Especially is this true with respect to common words. Therefore, this unit is designed as a means of insuring the proper form for sixty words whose pronunciation has caused consid·· erable difficulty. It is safe to say that not three persons in 500,000 can pronounce correctly the following list, known as "Gilmartin's Sixty Snags." Some of the words appear in following sections, but owing to their degree of difficulty a repetition of them should be worth while.

Try to pronounce the following list of words before you study the explanatory paragraphs which follow:

alias	chiropodist	salient
gaseous	appreciate	verbatim
infamous	epitome	imbroglio
grimace	mayoralty	virus
renege	poinsettia	irrevocable
respite	hosiery	hospitable
vanilla	remuneration	inexplicable
orgy	preferable	municipal
formidáble	mulattoes	puerile
genuine	machination	lamentable
dirigible	schism	longevity
derisive	fricassee	alumnae
arctic	posthumous	chastisement
autopsy	intricacy	sarsaparilla
irreparable	ultimatum	marshmallow
zoology	quietus	robot
auxiliary	credence	impotent
comely	maraschino	clandestine
heinous	frailty	boutonnierc
psychiatrist	Hawaii	impious

alias   **ay' lee us**, not **a lye' us**
    The first syllable rhymes with **say** and is accented.
    John Doe, **alias** Sam Black, was arrested.

gaseous   **gas' e us**, and not **gash' us**
    Too often is this word sounded with two syllables when it
      rightly demands three syllables.
    The talk related to **gaseous** matter.

3

infamous   in' fuh mus, not in fay' mus
Accent the first syllable and pronounce the second syllable **fuh.**
He has an **infamous** reputation.

grimace   grimace', not grim' is
This word, which means "a distortion of the countenance," has
two possible difficulties: the place of the accent, and the
sound of the last syllable. The syllable **mace** rhymes with
face and receives the accent.
His **grimaces** made the people laugh.

renege   reneeg', not renague
It is necessary to have this word rhyme with **league** and not
with **plague,** which is frequently heard.
He did not realize that he **reneged** during the game of cards.

respite   res' pit, not respite'
"A temporary suspension of labor or effort; an
interval of rest; delay."
Be sure to accent the first syllable and to have the last syllable
rhyme with **hit** and not with **kite.**
The executive seemed to get no **respite** from his troubles.

vanilla   vuh nil' uh, not vuh nel' uh.
Let the second syllable rhyme with **pill.**
She likes **vanilla** ice cream.

orgy   or' ji, not or' ghee
The modern meaning is "drunken revelry; excessive indulgence
in some activity." The **g** is sounded like **j** and not like the
g in **get.**
The students' **orgy** was occasioned by the football victory.

formidable   for' midable, not formid' able
"Hard to accomplish; difficult to overcome."
To pronounce this word correctly, accent the first syllable and
not the second.
He presented a **formidable** argument.

genuine   jen' u in, not jen' u ine
The last syllable should rhyme with **pin.**
This is a **genuine** diamond.

dirigible   dir' igible, not dirij' ible
Accent the first syllable and not the second which is too fre-
quently done.
A **dirigible** passed over our city at noon.

derisive   de rye' siv, not de riss' ive
"Ridiculing; mocking."
The second syllable should rhyme with **cry** and not with **miss.**
That **derisive** remark was unnecessary.

arctic   ark′ tic, not ar′ tic
> Let the first syllable rhyme with **bark** and not with **bar**.
> They are in the **Arctic** region.

Practice

1. How many syllables has **gaseous**?
2. Give the sound of the last syllable in **grimace**.
3. Explain the accent of the word **respite** and the sound of its second syllable.
4. How is the letter g in **orgy** sounded?
5. On what syllable is **alias** accented?
6. Give the sound of the second syllable in **derisive**.
7. What syllable in **vanilla** requires attention?

autopsy   au′ topsy, not autop′ sy
> The first syllable and not the second receives the accent.
> An **autopsy** was ordered to ascertain the cause of his death.

irreparable   irrep′ arable, not irrepair′ able
> "Not capable of being repaired or remedied."
> Accent the second syllable, not the third.
> **Irreparable** damage was caused by the fire.

zoology   zo ol′ o gy, not zoo ol′ o gy
> Do not associate the sound of the first syllable with **zoo**. It should rhyme with **flow**.
> He is interested in **zoology**.

auxiliary   og zil′ yuh re, not oz zil′ e ay re
> The correct pronunciation of this word contains four syllables and not five.
> **Auxiliary** troops soon appeared.

comely   kum′ ly, not comb′ ly
> "Pleasing to the sight."
> Sound the first syllable to rhyme with **drum** and not with **dome**.
> She was a **comely** person.

heinous   hay′ nus, not hee′ nus
> "Hateful; wicked."
> He committed a **heinous** crime.

psychiatrist   suh kye′ a trist, not syc′ ke a′ trist
> Attention should be focused upon the second syllable for accent and pronunciation.
> She was advised to consult a **psychiatrist**.

chiropodist   kye rop' o dist, not ker op' o dist or
sher op' o dist
"One who treats of ailments of the feet, especially
minor ailments."

Note that the first syllable is sounded to rhyme with **eye** and
not with **blur**.

The **chiropodist** said the trouble was caused by ill-fitting shoes.

appreciate   a pree' she ate, not a pree' see ate
Though many speakers pronounce the third syllable **see**, the
dictionaries advocate **she**.

They did not **appreciate** our services.

epitome   e pit' o me, not ep' itome
"A brief or curtailed statement of the contents
of a work."

If you have not read *Silas Marner,* at least acquaint yourself
with an **epitome** of the book.

mayoralty   may' or al ty, not may or al' i ty
"The position of mayor or his term of office."

This word is frequently mispronounced by giving it five syllables. It contains only four. Do not confuse it with the
pronunciation of **majority or plurality.**

poinsettia   poin set' ti a, not poin set' ta
The name of this flower, which is seen in great profusion during the Christmas season, must contain four and not three
syllables.

There was a **poinsettia** in every window.

hosiery   ho' zher y, not hose' er y
The second syllable of this word is pronounced as if spelled
zher.

She has bought some **hosiery.**

remuneration   re mew' ner ay' shun, not
re new' mer ay' shun
Note that the second syllable is **mu** and not **nu**. It is not
related to enumerate.

The **remuneration** was satisfactory to the actors.

Practice

1. Give the sound of the first syllable in: **comely; zoology; heinous.**

2. How many syllables are there in: **poinsettia; epitome;
auxiliary?**

3. What pronunciation difficulty is presented by: **hosiery**; **mayoralty**; **chiropodist**?

4. Use in sentences the noun and verb forms of: **appreciate**; **delegate**.

5. Where is the accent in: **epitome**; **autopsy**?

preferable   pref' er a ble, not pre fer' a ble
The first syllable should be accented.
With him play was **preferable** to work.

mulattoes   mu lat' oes, not ma lah' toes
The first syllable is **mu** not **ma**, and the second syllable rhymes with **bat** and not **bah**.
There are many **mulattoes** in this city.

machination   mak' a nay' shun, not mash' a nay' shun
"Evil or artful plotting."
Sound the first syllable **mak**, not **mash**.
The state's heavy indebtedness was attributed to the **machinations** of certain politicians.

schism   sizm, not skism or shizm
"A division in hostile groups."
A **schism** in their party caused their defeat.

fricassee   frik a see', not frig a see'
Note that the first syllable should rhyme with **brick** and not with **brig**.
She ordered chicken **fricassee**.

posthumous   pos' tew mus, not post hew' mus
"Published after death of author."
The book contains the **posthumous** letters of the poet.

intricacy   in' truh ka se, not in trick' a se
"Complicated; involved."
The **intricacy** of the plan frightened many of us.

ultimatum   ul ta may' tum, not ulta mah' tum
The third syllable should rhyme with **bay** and not with **rah**.
The latter is the Latin sound.
The country disregarded the dictator's **ultimatum**.

quietus   kwy ee' tus, not kwy' e tus
"The final settlement; anything which puts an end to action, as death."
Though this word is associated in meaning with **quiet**, its pronunciation bears no resemblance. One must accent the second syllable, which rhymes with **glee**.
Another week will put a **quietus** to my college career.

credence   kree' dence, not kred' ence
"Belief."
> The first syllable is **kree** to rhyme with **three**.
> Place no **credence** in that story.

maraschino   marr' a ske' no, not marr' a she' no
> The difficulty in this word rests in the sound of the third syllable. It is pronounced **skee**, not **shee**.
> Here is a bottle of **maraschino** cherries.

frailty   frail' ty, not fray' al ty
> Only two syllables are to be given this word.
> His greatest **frailty** was his dishonesty.

Hawaii   Hah wy' ee, not Ha wah' ee
> Sound the second syllable, **wai**, like the letter **y**, and you will have the correct pronunciation of this word.
> He is spending his vacation in **Hawaii**.

Practice

Fill each blank with an appropriate answer.

1. The first syllable in **credence** is sounded _____.
2. The sound of the second syllable in **mulattoes** is _____; in **quietus**, it is _____.
3. The third syllable in **maraschino** is pronounced _____.
4. **Salient** is a word of _____ syllables.
5. Attention should be given to the sound of the _____ syllable in **fricassee** and the _____ in **verbatim**.

salient   say' le ent, not sayl' yent
> This word, whether a noun or an adjective, should be pronounced with three syllables.
> That was the **salient** purpose of his visit.

verbatim   ver bay' tim, not ver bat' im
> This word, which was taken directly from the Latin, has its second syllable rhyme with **hay**.
> The magazine published the speech **verbatim**.

imbroglio   imbrol' yo, not im brog' li o or imbroil' yo
> "A complicated or confused situation; a serious misunderstanding."
> Be sure to limit this word to three syllables, and to have the second syllable rhyme with **sole**. The last is sounded **yo**.
> What was the cause of their **imbroglio**?

virus   vye' rus, not veer' us

In practically all English words which begin with **vir**, it is pronounced **veer**. But the first syllable in **virus** is **vi** and it is pronounced **vye**.

He is suffering from **virus** pneumonia.

irrevocable   irrev' ocable, not irrevoke' able

"Not to be withdrawn or annulled."

Accent the second syllable, not the third.

It was an **irrevocable** decision.

hospitable   hos' pitable, not hospit' able

"Liking to give welcome to guests; kind."

Accent the first and not the second syllable of this word.

They were very **hospitable** to us.

inexplicable   inex' plicable, not inexplic' able

"Not able to be explained."

Place the accent before the **plic** syllable.

The murder has remained an **inexplicable** mystery.

municipal   munis' ipal, not mu' nisipal

This word which belongs to the common variety should be accented on the second syllable and not on the first syllable.

We are most interested in **municipal** affairs.

puerile   pew' er il, not pure' il

"Childish; foolish."

Note that this word has three syllables the first of which should rhymo with **fcw**.

He presented a **puerile** argument.

lamentable   lam' entable, not lament' able

"Sad; mournful."

Note that the first syllable has the accent.

He related a **lamentable** story.

longevity   lon jev' i ty, not long gev' i ty

"Great length of life; the tendency to live long."

Let the first syllable **lon** rhyme with the **pon** in **pond** and give a **j** sound to the **g** in the second syllable.

He attributed his **longevity** to lack of worry.

Practice

1. Give the sound of the first syllable in **virus**.

2. How many syllables has **imbroglio**? Sound the second one.

3. Where is the accent in **hospitable**? In **inexplicable**?

4.   What difficulty is found in **irrevocable?**

5.   Which syllable is accented in **lamentable?**   In **incognito?**

alumnae   a lum′ nee, not a lum′ nye
>   The last syllable of this word which means "women graduates
>   or former students of a school or college" should rhyme with
>   **glee** and not with **cry.**   The latter is the Latin sound.   The
>   last syllable in the masculine form, **alumni,** rhymes with **cry.**
>   Many of the **alumnae** will attend the exercises.

chastisement   chas′ tizment, not chastize′ ment
>   Though this word derives its meaning from **chastise,** its pro-
>   nunciation is not related to the verb form.   Accent the first
>   syllable.
>   He received a merited **chastisement** for his mistake.

sarsaparilla   sar″ sa pa ril′ a, not sars″ pa ril′ a or
>   sas pa rel′ a
>   Note that this word has five syllables, each of which should be
>   distinctly sounded.
>   We drank some **sarsaparilla.**

marshmallow   marsh′ mal″ o, not marsh mahl′ o or
>   marsh mel′ o
>   The second syllable **mal** should rhyme with **pal** and not with
>   **doll** or **sell.**
>   The girls toasted **marshmallows.**

robot   row′ bot or rob′ ot, but not row′ bo
>   "A machine constructed in human form, hence a
>   person who works mechanically."
>   Many, thinking that this word is a French word, do not sound
>   the final **t.**   It is of Czech origin, and the last syllable is
>   sounded almost like **it.**
>   A **robot** directs traffic.

impotent   im′ potent, not impo′ tent
>   "Not having power; helpless."
>   Do not associate its pronunciation with **potent;** if you do, you
>   will not accent the proper syllable, which is the first.
>   The leader was **impotent** against such a large number of the
>   enemy.

clandestine   klan des′ tin, not klan′ duh steen
>   "Secret; concealed; hidden."
>   Accent the second syllable and there will be no pronunciation
>   difficulty.
>   It was a **clandestine** marriage.

boutonniere   boo″ to nyar′
"A flower or bouquet worn in the buttonhole."
Note that this is a word of three and not four syllables; also
that the accent is *not* on the second syllable. The last syllable rhymes with **rare.**

impious   im′ pee us, not im pye′ us
"Wicked; lacking piety."
The first syllable is accented and the second syllable rhymes
with **key.**
The destruction of the church was an **impious** act.

Practice

Correct if necessary:

1. **Clandestine** is accented on the second syllable.
2. You may say **impo′ tent.**
3. There are five syllables in **sarsaparilla.**
4. The form **chastise′ ment** is incorrect.
5. Always accent the second syllable in **impious.**
6. One should never say **marshmellow.**
7. The last syllable in **alumnae** may be pronounced to rhyme with either **see** or **fly.**
8. The **t** in **robot** is not silent.
9. Always accent the first syllable in **impotent.**
10. One may say **row′ bot** or **rob′ ot.**

Pronunciation Changes

A study of the Webster's New Collegiate Dictionary, published in 1949, revealed that several words, hitherto restricted to one correct pronunciation, have received added pronunciations which must be accepted. There are many people who think that the adoption of a certain pronunciation is the result of the arbitrary choice of the dictionary editors. This is far from being true. The dictionary makers simply record that form which is and has been used by a great number of people throughout the country for a period of years. The pronunciation that is characteristic of or limited to a particular section does not receive the sanction of the editors nor does it merit a place in their book.

The following words, since the publication of Webster's New Collegiate Dictionary, possess multiple pronunciations.

quay
It will be delightful news to all word students to know that **quay** in addition to its always correct pronunciation, **key**, which was practically impossible to explain, may also be pronounced, **qway.**

clique
Though the majority of people seemed to pronounce this word, **click**, there was no dictionary authority to substantiate it. The form, **cleek**, which was advocated by all dictionaries is still preferred, but to say **click** is no longer incorrect.

cerebral
For years many doctors, patients, and others persisted in pronouncing this word, **suh ree' bral,** though no authoritative source could be furnished for it. That pronunciation is now labeled correct. The form **ser' uh bral** is, however, preferred.

aviation
All dictionaries concurred in having the first syllable of this word pronounced **ay** to rhyme with **bay.** A secondary pronunciation now permits **av** to be the sound of the first syllable. **Aviator** is likewise affected.

forehead
The secondary pronunciation sanctions the sounding of the letter **h.** **For' ed** is the preferred form; **for' hed** is secondary.

digitalis
Why the form **dij a tay' lis** remained the only accepted pronunciation would be difficult to state. The majority of people seemed to say, **dij a tal' is,** the third syllable rhyming with **pal.** That pronunciation is now preferred to **dij a tay' lis.**

Pronunciation Changes

culinary

To sound the first syllable like the letter **q** was formerly the only correct form. One is now permitted to pronounce the first syllable **cul** to rhyme with **dull**. The latter is the secondary pronunciation.

applicable

For decades, words that contained **plic** or **pic** as the second syllable were never accented on that syllable. The accent was placed on the preceding syllable. But if a student now says, **applic′ able**, he is using the form recorded as secondary in the dictionary. **Ap′ plicable** is still the preferred pronunciation. This change also characterizes the pronunciation of **explicable** and **despicable**.

impetigo

If the skin disease is called **im pe tee′ go**, this pronunciation is no longer incorrect. The preferred form is **im pe tye′ go**.

status

This is one of the many words whose Latin spelling was adopted by our language and which have received secondary pronunciations. **Stay′ tus** is the preferred form; **stat′ us** is the secondary form. Less than two decades ago the Latin-spelled words **data, stratum, gratis, apparatus** and others received secondary pronunciations.

khaki

The form **kock′ ey** to rhyme with **jockey** was the only pronunciation found in the dictionaries. To have **khaki** rhyme with **lackey** is now permissible as the secondary pronunciation.

gardenia

Formerly it was necessary to pronounce this word as one of four syllables, **gahr dee′ ne a.** A recorded secondary form is **gahr dee′ nya.**

syringe

The student is no longer restricted to placing the accent on the first syllable of this word, whether it is a noun or a verb. To accent the last syllable is the secondary form.

entirety

Though most people always pronounced this word as one of four syllables, they could name no dictionary to justify that pronunciation. Now, **en tire′ ty** is first; **en tye′ ret y** is second.

precedence

A large segment of the population will be happy to learn that **pre see′ dense** is not the only pronunciation for this word. A secondary form, **pres′ e dense**, is new found in the dictionary.

171 Vocabulary Builders

1

Words Often Confused

You will note that the words in the following pairs, while they may be similar in pronunciation, have altogether different meanings.

principal (*n.*) One who takes a leading part; a head of a school; a sum of money.

principle A general truth; a rule of conduct.

Read aloud: The **principals** in the show displayed excellent talent.

The **principal** of the school was injured.

We must instill into the minds of our youth **principles** of honesty and obedience.

council An assembly or group for conference.

counsel Advice; a legal adviser.

Read aloud: The decision demanded a meeting of the **council**.

The youth refused to follow the **counsel** of his parents.

My **counsel** has advised me to answer no questions relative to the case.

capital A chief city; a sum of money.

capitol A statehouse.

Read aloud: Albany is the **capital** of New York.

We have insufficient **capital** for that great project.

The dome of the **Capitol** at Washington, D. C., is being renovated.

mantel A shelf above a fireplace.

mantle A cloak.

Read aloud: The clock was placed on the **mantel**.

The actor threw the **mantle** over his shoulder.

Reorganization may be a **mantle** to cloak the handout of jobs as election rewards.

stationary Not moving; fixed.

stationery Writing paper.

Read aloud: The desks in this room are **stationary**.

I received a box of **stationery** yesterday.

Practice

1. Use in sentences: **capitalize; counselled.**

2. Construct sentences with the adjectives: **principal; capital.**

2

Related Words *(fuse)*

infuse
To pour in; to instill, as principles and qualities; to inspire or imbue.
(The accent is on the last syllable: **in fuz′**.)
Read aloud: The teacher **infused** his love of Latin into the minds of his students.
Legislation that will **infuse** confidence into the minds of the people is needed.

suffuse
To overspread, as with a liquid; to fill, as with something fluid.
(Note the sound of the last syllable: **su fuz′**.)
Read aloud: Her eyes were **suffused** with tears.
An expression of confidence **suffused** their faces.

diffuse *(v.)*
To cause to flow on all sides; to spread; to circulate; to scatter; to dissipate.
(The pronunciation of the verb is **di fuz′**.)
Read aloud: He **diffused** good feelings wherever he went.
His mission in life was to **diffuse** knowledge among the poor.

The adjective, **diffuse**, means "widespread; scattered; not concentrated; copious; full." Note the pronunciation: **di fus′**. The last syllable of the adjective rhymes with **abuse**, the noun; the last syllable of the verb rhymes with **muse**.
Read aloud: He was **diffuse** in his interests.
Brown is a man of **diffuse** knowledge.

profuse *(adj.)*
Pouring forth liberally; excessively generous in giving or spending; prodigal; lavish.
(The last syllable rhymes with the noun **use**: **pro fus′**.)
Read aloud: He was **profuse** in his apologies.
The stream of **profuse** spending must be dammed.

Practice

1. Construct sentences with: **diffusive; profusion.**

2. Use in sentences the noun form of: **infuse; diffuse.**

3

Adjectives

One cannot overstress the importance of the use of adjectives and adverbs in oral or written speech. It has often been said that an orator or writer is judged by his use of appropriate adjectives and adverbs. Begin at once to garner your supply of these words which will prove most useful to you in the future.

animated   Full of life or spirit; vigorous.
> *Read aloud:* There was an **animated** discussion about politics at the club.
> In an **animated** tone he prescribed a remedy for the existing ills of society.
> The two colleges took part in an **animated** debate.
> *Use in sentences:* **animated** expression; **animated** description; **animated** quarrel; **animated** sounds.

lashing   Striking forcibly and quickly; berating or censuring with words.
> *Read aloud:* Such **lashing** sarcasm was uncalled for.
> He received a **lashing** rebuke for his negligence.
> The New Deal suffered constantly the **lashing** editorials of the Republican newspapers.

tenable   Capable of being held, maintained, or defended, as against an assailant or objector. (There are two pronunciations for this word: **ten′ a ble** and **tee′ na ble**.)
> *Read aloud:* The argument he presented was **tenable**.
> The army's position was not **tenable**.

Practice

1. Place in sentences: **animate** (*v.*); **animation**.

2. Write three synonyms for: **tenable**; **animated** (*adj.*); **lashing**.

4

Adjectives Ending in *tory*

If you listen attentively to the diction of outstanding orators, you will detect many euphonious adjectives. Some of these will end in **tory**. Familiarize yourself with the following adjectives having that suffix so as to be able to use them in your written or oral work.

confirmatory   Serving to verify; corroborative.

(It is now permissible to place a secondary accent on the fourth syllable **to** in all the **tory** words. Formerly one had to say: **confirm′ atory**; now it is correct to say: **confirm′ ato″ ry**.)

Read aloud: I am awaiting a letter **confirmatory** of that order.

There was a **confirmatory** expression on his countenance when I finished my speech.

What **confirmatory** proof have we that peace is their primary objective?

dedicatory   Constituting or serving as a dedication.

(The primary accent is on the first syllable, and the secondary accent is on the fourth syllable: **ded′ icato″ ry**.)

Read aloud: Rain fell heavily during the **dedicatory** exercises.

The **dedicatory** speech at Gettysburg was delivered by Edward Everett.

condemnatory   Condemning; containing or imposing condemnation or censure.

Read aloud: His talk was full of **condemnatory** phrases relative to the weaknesses of our educational system.

He apparently received the **condemnatory** sentence with resignation.

Practice

1. Use in sentences the noun form of: **confirmatory; condemnatory.**

2. Construct sentences with the adjectives: **confirmed; confirmable.**

5

Words for Your Vocabulary

infallible   Not capable of erring; not liable to fail, deceive, or disappoint; certain.
Read aloud: Only God is **infallible.**
His conscience proved an **infallible** guide.
He really thinks that he is **infallibly** guided in his political work.

commodious   Roomy; adapted to wants and necessities.
(The second syllable is **mo,** not **mod,** and is pronounced to rhyme with **glow.**)
Read aloud: We had a well-located, **commodious** room at the hotel.
The site was not **commodious** enough for a college.

astute   Shrewd; wise; crafty; clever.
(The accent is placed on the last syllable: **astute'.**)
Read aloud: He is, indeed, an **astute** lawyer.
The **astute** answers given to the judge were published in the newspapers.
He **astutely** waited until he was sure of victory.

harass   To fatigue; to trouble by repeated attacks; to disturb.
(You may pronounce this word in two ways: either **har'** as or **harass'.**)
Read aloud: Do not **harass** me with so many questions.
He was much **harassed** by his ever-increasing debts.
Weak nations are being **harassed** by military states desirous of greater wealth and power.

Practice

1. Construct sentences with: **fallible; fallibility; fallacy.**

2. Give three synonyms for: **astute; commodious.**

19

6

Pronunciation

A knowledge of the words in the "Pronunciation" sections will effect a twofold good: it will enhance your word supply and will add solidarity and confidence to your pronunciation. The first two words on this page have received secondary pronunciations.

despicable   des′ picable or despic′ able
              Fit or deserving to be despised; contemptible.

   Read aloud: It was **despicable** to refuse food to the hungry old man.

   He was reprimanded for his **despicable** language.

secretive   sekree′ tive or see′ kretive
              Disposed to keep secrets; not frank or open; extremely reticent.

   Read aloud: An efficient secretary should be a **secretive** person.

   Dictators work in a **secretive** and inhuman way.

chastisement   (chas′ tizment)
               Punishment; discipline; pain inflicted to punish or correct.

Because **advertisement** has two pronunciations, one must not deduce that **chastisement** must also have two correct forms: it has but one correct pronunciation. The accent is on the first syllable. Do not say **chastize′ ment.**

   Read aloud: The **chastisement** was really undeserved.

   The indulgent parent found it difficult to inflict any **chastisement** upon his unruly child.

Practice

1. Can you think of three adjectives whose second syllable is **plic**?

2. How many correct pronunciations has **advertisement?**

3. What is the verb form of: **despicable; secretive?**

Words for Your Vocabulary

inveigh To make a violent attack in words; to reproach.
(Pronounce this word **in vay'**.)
Read aloud: They **inveighed** against the overwhelming debt
of the country.
The public **inveighed** against the lack of police protection
for the city.

urgency Need for immediate attention or action; insistence.
Read aloud: During the flood there was a great **urgency**
for food.
The **urgency** of new legislation is manifesting itself in every
state.

abhor To shrink away from with horror; to feel exces-
sive dislike toward; to detest extremely.
(Accent the last syllable of this word.)
Read aloud: She literally **abhors** mice.
The fastidious teacher **abhorred** the use of slang.

mediate To effect a reconciliation or agreement; to be a
go-between; to bring about a settlement or
agreement.
(The pronunciation is **mee' di ate.** The first
syllable rhymes with **glee.**)
Read aloud: We tried to **mediate** a peace between the con-
flicting parties.
The attempt to **mediate** a compromise between the strikers
and employers failed.

Practice

Use these synonyms for **abhor** in sentences: **detest; loathe;
abominate.**

8

Adjectives

facile
Fluent; quick; free in performing or expressing; moving with ease.

(This word is accented on the first syllable and is pronounced **fas′ il**.)

Read aloud: Many books have come from his **facile** pen.

His **facile** nature enabled him to be content with any company.

To be a recognized conversationalist, one must possess a **facile** tongue.

Use in sentences: **facile ruler; facile methods; facile command; facile hand.**

tacit
Silent; implied or indicated; unspoken; wordless.

Read aloud: He received my **tacit** consent to go to the ball game.

His **tacit** gesture quieted the noisy youngster.

That act will surely merit the **tacit** disapproval of your family.

Use in sentences: **tacit obedience; tacit support; tacit ownership; tacit approval.**

virile
Having the qualities or properties of an adult man; masterful; forceful; showing vigor.

(This word may be pronounced **veer′ il** or **vye′ rl**.)

Read aloud: To convince the opposition was a **virile** undertaking.

He made a **virile** attempt to save the drowning person.

A **virile** hand is needed to pilot our course.

Use in sentences: **virile achievement; virile leader; virile denunciation; virile legislation.**

Practice

Construct sentences with: **facility; virility.**

Words for Your Vocabulary

frugal   Economical; without waste; saving; using things well.

(Do not associate the idea of "stinginess" with this word.)

Read aloud: To make both ends meet, we shall have to live **frugally.**

Their **frugal** methods were worthy of imitation.

Have they completely forgotten that **frugal** spending will eventually lighten the load?

digress   To turn aside; to deviate from the main subject either in writing or in speaking.

(Remember to accent this word on the last syllable: **digress'.** The i in **di** may be short like the i in **pin** or long like the i in **ice.**)

Read aloud: The speaker **digressed** too much from the subject.

One should not **digress** from the laws of nature.

irresolute   Wavering; not decided or determined; hesitating.

Read aloud: The **irresolute** ruler hastened the revolution.

He was **irresolute** in his management of the business.

inveigle   To lead astray by deceiving; to allure; to entice.

(This word may be pronounced correctly in two ways: **invee' gle** or **invay' gle.**)

Read aloud: We were **inveigled** into buying some worthless stock.

Instead of attending school, he was **inveigled** into a theatrical career.

Practice

1. Use in sentences: **digressive; frugality.**
2. What is the stem word of **irresolute?**

Self-Check No. One

Selection Exercise

Choose the form of the word in parentheses which makes the sentence correct:

1. He did not follow his father's (**council, counsel**).
2. A (**mantle, mantel**) of snow covered the ground.
3. He is a man of high (**principal, principle**).
4. The box of (**stationery, stationary**) is on the table.
5. He (**councilled, counseled**) us against being ungrateful.
6. What was his (**principle, principal**) objection?
7. The legislature met in the (**capitol, capital**) at Albany.

True and False

Correct the statements which are incorrect:

1. **Harass** must be accented on the first syllable.
2. The second syllable of **secretive** is pronounced **kree**.
3. **Chastisement** has only one correct pronunciation.
4. **Despicable** is accented on the first syllable.
5. The adjective **diffuse** rhymes with **fuse**.
6. **Virile** must be pronounced **veer′ il**.
7. **Inveigle** must not be pronounced **invay′ gle**.

Sentences and Expressions

1. Construct sentences with:
    infuse   infallible   abhor   astute   urgency
2. Have each adjective modify two nouns:
    profuse   lashing   animated   despicable   confirmatory
3. Give the noun forms of:
    frugal   facile   virile   digress   diffuse

10

Words Often Confused

roster	A roll or list.
rostrum	A stage for public speaking; the pulpit or platform used by an orator.

Read aloud: Glenn Cunningham, phenomenal miler and middle-distance ace, headed the **roster** of contestants.

As the speaker approached the **rostrum**, there was absolute silence in the audience.

egoism	Excessive thought and love of self; the habit of regarding oneself as the center of every interest.
egotism	The practice of speaking or writing overmuch of oneself; self-praise.

(No doubt the real difference between these two words is that **egoism** is ascribed to a person who is passive and thinks much of himself; **egotism** is ascribed to one who not only thinks much of self, but who also gives expression, either in speaking or writing, to this high esteem in which he holds himself.)

Read aloud: Though Smith is quiet, he possesses a great amount of **egoism**.

The **egotism** of the orator was nauseating.

deprecate	To express disapproval of.
depreciate	To lessen in price or value; to lower the worth of; to belittle.

Read aloud: He **deprecated** the use of slang.

The proposed bill was **deprecated** by many Congressmen.

Real estate has **depreciated** greatly during the past few years.

Some slaves **depreciated** the value of freedom.

Practice

1. Place in sentences: **ego**; **egotistic**.

2. Give two antonyms for **egotistic**. (An *antonym* is an opposite.)

11

Related Words *(cred)*

Frequently a knowledge of one word may pave the way to the acquisition of other words that belong to the same family.

Let us take the word **credit**. It is derived from the Latin **credo,** which means *I believe.* If you analyze the simple word **credit,** you will note its relationship to its parent word, for you cannot receive **credit** unless the person with whom you are doing business believes that you will ultimately pay. Hence, through all words derived from **credo** you will observe the same thread of meaning pertinent to *belief.*

Here are a few words of the **credo** family. Definitions and illustrations will be given for them.

credence   Belief; trust, confidence.
(To pronounce this word correctly, you must say **kree′ dense.** The first syllable is **kree,** to rhyme with **plea,** not **kred,** rhyming with **bread.)**
Read aloud: I placed no **credence** in what he said.
She gives too much **credence** to gossip.

credible   Worthy of belief; capable of being believed.
(The first syllable is pronounced **kred.)**
Read aloud: It was a **credible** story he told.
The information we received was **credible.**

incredible   Surpassing belief; unlikely; marvelous.
Read aloud: He told an **incredible** fish story.
The car travels with **incredible** speed.

credulous   Apt to believe on slight evidence; easily imposed upon.
Read aloud: Old people are inclined to be **credulous.**
One should not be too **credulous.**

Practice

Illustrate in sentences the meaning of: **credo; credentials· creditable; incredulous.**

26

12

Adjectives

vigorous   Full of physical or mental strength or active force; strong; enforced rigidly.

Read aloud: A **vigorous** attempt was made to repeal the law.

A **vigorous** recovery began during the winter months.

The citizens made a **vigorous** protest against the actions of certain officials.

Use in sentences: **vigorous plea; vigorous denial; vigorous enforcement; vigorous speaker.**

valid   Founded on truth or fact; efficient; effective; capable of being supported or defended.

Read aloud: The people presented a **valid** objection to the place.

The youngster could not give the policemen a **valid** excuse for being out so late.

The document was found to be **valid.**

Use in sentences: **valid argument; valid agreement; valid claim; valid contract.**

audible   Capable of being heard; actually heard; loud enough to be heard.

(Let the first syllable of this word, **au,** sound like the **o** in **orb.**)

Read aloud: His speech was hardly **audible** to those in the rear of the hall.

The girls spoke in **audible** whispers.

Practice

1. Construct sentences with: **invigorate; validity; validate; invalidate.**

2. Use the following synonyms for **vigorous** in sentences: **forcible; strenuous; vehement.**

13

Adjectives Ending in *al*

In Latin it was customary to add **alis** to the noun stem in order to form an adjective. When we add the suffix **al** to form an adjective, it has the meaning *pertaining to, like,* or *appropriate to.* These words contain the suffix **al.**

regal   Belonging to a king; royal; fit for kings; stately; splendid.

Read aloud: The soldiers received a **regal** welcome on their return to America.

The guests were dressed in **regal** splendor.

In acting as he did, he was usurping **regal** power.

pastoral   Pertaining to shepherds; relating to rural life and scenes; also, expressive of the life of shepherds. (The accent is on the first syllable: **pas′ toral.**)

Read aloud: We enjoyed the **pastoral** scenery of Ireland.

There was **pastoral** music all through the play.

He prefers a **pastoral** life to one of business.

tragical   Tragic; having the manner, style, or spirit of tragedy; doleful; sad.

Read aloud: The young men met a **tragical** death in their new airplane.

The actor had a **tragical** look.

The play was too **tragical** for me to enjoy it.

temporal   Lasting for time only; of this life only; civil or political, as distinguished from ecclesiastical.

Read aloud: Too many are attracted by the **temporal** pleasures of this world.

Let the goal be a lasting and not merely a **temporal** relief.

Practice

Construct sentences with: **extemporize; extemporaneous.**

The King's Library

14

Words for Your Vocabulary

emolument   Profit from office, labor, or employment; compensation; fees or salary.
Read aloud: The **emoluments** of his political position enabled him to purchase a palatial residence.
That his people were satisfied with his rule was sufficient **emolument** for him.

capricious   Apt to change suddenly; guided by one's fancy; whimsical; irregular.
Read aloud: Her **capricious** nature was exasperating.
It was difficult to become accustomed to the **capricious** climate of New England.

subsidize   To help or assist with a contribution of money; to aid, as a private enterprise, with public money.
Read aloud: The rioters were **subsidized** by enemy-aliens.
The steamship line was **subsidized** by the government.

peremptory   Decisive; final; absolute; essential; imperious; positive.
(You may pronounce this word in two ways: **peremp' tory** or **per' empto" ry**.)
Read aloud: He was too **peremptory** to be successful.
His **peremptory** orders were always carried out.
His answer was a **peremptory** "No!"

herculean   Of great strength, courage, or size; very hard to do.
(There are two correct pronunciations for this word: **hercu' lean** and **her" culee' an**. The **cu** is pronounced like the letter **q**.)
Read aloud: He was a man of **herculean** strength.
To quell the tumult was a **herculean** task.

Practice

What are the noun forms of: **subsidize; capricious?**

29

Pronunciation

penalize   pee' nalize or pen' alize
To put a penalty on; to punish; to handicap.

The first syllable may now be prounounced **pee** or **pen**.

Read aloud: He was **penalized** for driving without a license.
The football team was **penalized** five yards for offside play.
Why **penalize** the public because of one man's shortsightedness?

applicable   ap' plicable or applic' able
Capable of being applied; fit, suitable, or right to
be applied.

This word is now in the category of words with two recorded pronunciations. Either the first or second syllable may
be accented.

Read aloud: What I said was **applicable** to the importance of
word study.
The letter was **applicable** to the case that was being tried.

hospitable   (hos' pitable)
Receiving and entertaining guests generously and
kindly; liberally receptive.

Note that the first syllable, **hos,** and not the second syllable,
pit, receives the accent. Never say **hospit' able.**

Read aloud: We found them **hospitable** people.
He is a person who is **hospitable** to the ideas of others.

inhospitable   (inhos' pitable)
Unfriendly; not making visitors comfortable.

You will observe that this word is accented on **hos** the same
as its antonym. Do not say **inhospit' able.**

Read aloud: In all our travels, we never received **inhospitable**
treatment.
His **inhospitable** nature made him unpopular.

Practice
Use in sentences: **penal; inapplicable.**

16

Adjectives

ungovernable Not capable of being governed, ruled, or restrained; wild; unbridled.
Read aloud: His **ungovernable** temper cost him his position.
He wrote with an **ungovernable** pen.
Such **ungovernable** vehemence was not expected from the professor.
Use in sentences: **ungovernable tongue; ungovernable mob; ungovernable passion; ungovernable official.**

repugnant Distasteful; offensive; contradictory; irreconcilable; repulsive.
Read aloud: Study is something **repugnant** to the average pupil.
To contribute to charity was **repugnant** to Scrooge's method of reasoning.
Never would he commit an act that was **repugnant** to his country's honor.
Use in sentences: **repugnant properties; repugnant taste; repugnant characteristics; repugnant look.**

dormant Sleeping; inactive; quiet as if asleep.
Read aloud: Many animals are **dormant** during the winter.
The question remained **dormant** for many years.
Our **dormant** antagonism was aroused by his speech.
Use in sentences: **dormant possibilities; dormant fortune; dormant passions; dormant claim.**

Practice

Use in sentences: **latent; dormancy; repugnance; pugnacious.**

Adjectives Ending in *tory*

obligatory   Binding in law or conscience; imposing duty.
(This word has two correct pronunciations: the primary accent may be placed on the first or on the second syllable. A secondary accent is placed on the fourth syllable: **oblig′ ato″ ry** or **ob′ ligato″ ry**.)

Read aloud: Attendance at the conference was **obligatory** for every member.

To be able to discipline well is **obligatory** for a successful teacher.

conciliatory   Tending to conciliate, win over, or reconcile; pacific.
(In pronouncing this word, do not neglect to give it six syllables. Many people have fallen into the error of calling it **concilatory,** omitting the second **i.** The correct form is **con cil′ i a to″ ry.**)

Read aloud: **Conciliatory** measures were employed to avert a strike.

The manager is not in a very **conciliatory** mood today.

preparatory   Making ready; introducing; undergoing training or instruction.
(The primary accent is placed on the second syllable, and the secondary accent on the fourth syllable: **prepar′ ato″ ry.**)

Read aloud: There are many **preparatory** schools in our country.

He has done much **preparatory** work on his speech.

The adverb, **preparatory:**

Read aloud: **Preparatory** to his election, he promised to make my brother his secretary.

Practice

1. Construct sentences with the verb form of: **conciliatory; obligatory.**

2. Use in sentences: **reconcile; conciliation.**

18

Words for Your Vocabulary

supersede To take the place of; to force out of use as in-
ferior; to render obsolete; to supplant.
(Note that the last syllable of this word is spelled
sede. Never spell this word **supercede**.)
Read aloud: This order will **supersede** all previous orders.
The automobile has **superseded** the horse and buggy.
The mayor **superseded** Mr. Brown with Mr. Whitman.

conform To make like; to act according to law or rule;
to be in accord or harmony; to comply.
(The preposition that follows **conform** is usually
to or **with**.)
Read aloud: His religious beliefs do not **conform** with mine.
Our political principles should **conform** to those of George
Washington.

corruptible Capable of being changed for the worse; capable
of being bribed; perishable.
Read aloud: Not all politicians are **corruptible**.
That man's body is **corruptible** cannot be successfully denied.

stringent Strict in requirements; rigid; severe; characterized by scarcity of money to be loaned.
Read aloud: The laws against fast driving should be made
more **stringent**.
The **stringent** stock market of 1932 caused many failures.

Practice

1. Construct sentences with: **corrupt** (*v.*); **corruption**.

2. Have **stringent** qualify three different nouns.

Self-Check No. Two

Completion Exercise

applicable
audible
capricious
conciliatory
corruptible
credible
credulous

dormant
emolument
herculean
hospitable
incredulous
obligatory
penalized
peremptory

repugnant
stringent
subsidized
temporal
ungovernable
valid
vigorous

Fill each blank with a word from the above list:

1. We received _____ treatment from them.
2. Their voices were scarcely _____.
3. What he said was _____ to labor.
4. A(n) _____ protest was made by the people.
5. He presented a(n) _____ contract.
6. The team was _____ for offside play.
7. It is not _____ to do this work.
8. He at least told a(n) _____ story.
9. The youngster has _____ possibilities.
10. The thought of school is _____ to him.
11. His _____ commands were obeyed.
12. He is so _____ that he will believe that story.
13. The laws should be made more _____.
14. The people were not in a(n) _____ mind.
15. He is a man of _____ strength.

Questions

1. How does **egoism** differ from **egotism**?
2. Has **applicable** more than one correct pronunciation?
3. Is it ever correct to say **pen' alize**?
4. Can you think of two synonyms for **corruptible**?
5. What is the meaning of **deprecate**?

19

Words Often Confused

complement   Something which completes or makes perfect; number required to fill.

compliment   Something good said about one; something said in praise of one's work.

Read aloud: The army at present lacks its **complement** of men.

I received a **compliment** from the professor for my excellent examination mark.

aggravate   To make worse or more severe; to make more offensive; to intensify.

exasperate   To excite or inflame the anger of; to embitter. (Do not use **aggravate** in the sense of *to make angry.* Such usage has not yet been sanctioned as good English by the dictionary makers.)

Read aloud: If you go out in the rain, you may **aggravate** your cold.

Such self-pity is bound to **aggravate** your woes.

I was **exasperated** at his numerous demands for money.

We were unable to **exasperate** our adversaries.

purpose (*v.*)   To determine upon; to intend; to resolve to do or bring about.

propose   To set before the mind; to offer for consideration.

Read aloud: I **purpose** to write his biography this year.

They **proposed** terms of peace.

Practice

1. What is the meaning of the word **supplement**? How do you distinguish it from the word **complement**?

2. Write three synonyms for **exasperate**.

20

Pronunciation

credence   (kree' dens)
Belief; usually, belief formed lightly on the basis
of indirect testimony.

It is necessary to pronounce the first syllable **kree,** to rhyme
with **glee** and not with **fled.**

Read aloud: Place no **credence** in that report.
Too much **credence** was given the story.

status   stay' tus or stat' us
State or condition of a person; position of affairs;
social or professional standing.

This word, adopted entirely from the Latin, has two Anglicized pronunciations. The first syllable may be pronounced
stay or **stat.** To have it rhyme with **ma** is Latin and has not
yet been recognized by the makers of dictionaries.

Read aloud: With excessive borrowing in good years and bankruptcy or revolution in poor ones, the financial **status** of
the Caribbean countries has been deplorable.
As a lawyer, diplomat, and able politician, he did much to
raise the **status** of his race.

clandestine   (klandes' tin)
Conducted with secrecy by design, usually for an
evil purpose; concealed; underhand.

If you accent the second syllable, **des,** and not the last syllable, you will find no difficulty with this word. Do not say
klan de steen'.

Read aloud: The **clandestine** meeting took place in New York.
Nothing good resulted from their **clandestine** act.

Practice

1. Use in sentences: **status; clandestinely.**

2. Look up the pronunciation of: **strata; gratis.**

21

Synonyms

In the following words you will be able to see a similarity in meaning. Construct original sentences with the various words and read them aloud.

obstinate   Stubborn; not giving in.
> *Read aloud:* We found her idiotically **obstinate** toward acting in her own behalf.
> His **obstinate** determination hastened his ruin.

refractory   Obstinate; unmanageable; difficult to fuse.
> *Read aloud:* The **refractory** boy received a merited rebuke.
> It was difficult to ride the **refractory** horse.

inflexible   Firm; rigid.
> *Read aloud:* We demanded an **inflexible** promise from our employer.
> The wood was too **inflexible** for use in a bow.
> He was **inflexibly** firm in his refusal.

obdurate   Unyielding; not repentant; hardened in feelings; hard-hearted.
> *Read aloud:* The governor was **obdurate** in his refusal to intercede for the prisoner.
> The **obdurate** criminal was sentenced to prison for a long term.

intractable   Hard to manage; stubborn.
> *Read aloud:* That mule often became **intractable**.
> Such **intractable** soldiers had to be punished.

opinionated   Obstinate with regard to one's opinions; dogmatic.
> *Read aloud:* He was too **opinionated** to be popular.
> Some of the Senators were so **opinionated** that they would not listen to the other side of the argument.

Practice

Construct sentences with: **obstinacy; infraction.**

Adjectives

radical   Pertaining to the root or origin; fundamental original; extreme.

Read aloud: He had a **radical** dislike for the movies.

Radical changes were made at the factory during the summer.

A **radical** is one who would uproot and rebuild along completely different lines.

Use in sentences: **radical error; radical ideas; radical reforms; radical demands.**

merited   Deserved; due; just; praiseworthy.

Read aloud: **Merited** praise was lavished upon him for his victory.

It was a **merited** rebuke for his arrogance.

Those who do good receive a **merited** reward in the form of a clear conscience.

Use in sentences: **merited censure; merited honors; merited punishment; merited promotion.**

cardinal   Chief; fundamental; principal; of basic importance.

Read aloud: Honesty was his **cardinal** asset.

His **cardinal** weakness was laziness.

The **cardinal** objection to the project was presented by the women of the neighborhood.

Use in sentences: **cardinal grievance; cardinal principle; cardinal fault; cardinal virtue.**

Practice

Use in sentences: **eradicate; meritorious.**

23

Words for Your Vocabulary

fatuous   Foolish; silly; stupid.
(This word has no connection with the word **fat**.)
Read aloud: He always seems to be making **fatuous** remarks.
It was **fatuous** of him to think that he could fight a man thirty pounds heavier than he.
The Social Security Act has been derided in some quarters as a **fatuous** attempt to relieve the aged poor.

obliterate   To blot out; to remove all traces of; to remove utterly by any means.
(In pronouncing this word, be sure to make the first syllable **ob** and not **o**.)
Read aloud: He would like to **obliterate** all thoughts of the crime.
The rain **obliterated** the footprints.
Try as they may, his adversaries will never be able to **obliterate** the good he has done.

vehemence   Forcefulness; violence; fury; strong feeling.
Read aloud: There was much **vehemence** in his talk about the laxity of the police.
He is a speaker of great **vehemence**.
He **vehemently** denied having any connection with the meeting.

puerile   Childish, as contrasted with mature; foolish; unworthy of an adult.
(Pronounce this word as though it were spelled **pew′ er ill**. Note well the sound of the first syllable.)
Read aloud: To be sure, it was a **puerile** thing to try to run an automobile on such a small salary.
His **puerile** remarks detracted greatly from his speech.

Practice

1. Place in sentences: **vehement; vehemently.**
2. Give a synonym for: **fatuous; puerile.**

24

Related Words (*luster*)

Have you ever tried to count the number of words associated with **luster,** which means *shine, sheen,* or *gloss?* You have, however, often unknowingly used words based on this word. Let us dwell for a few moments on the following:

luster   Quality of shining with a self-originated light; radiance of beauty or renown; distinction.

Read aloud: The **luster** of her eye quickly disappeared when she received the sad news of her brother's death.

The toy soon lost its **luster** for the little fellow.

Such an achievement will unquestionably add **luster** to his name.

illustrious   Characterized by greatness or nobleness; famous; eminent.

Read aloud: Grant and Lee were **illustrious** generals.

We like to read of the **illustrious** deeds of our Revolutionary heroes.

lustrous   Shining; having luster; hence, radiant; illustrious.

Read aloud: We admired her **lustrous** hair.

His **lustrous** deeds speak for themselves.

Practice

1. How many spellings has **luster**?

2. **Illustrate** may be pronounced in how many ways?

3. Construct sentences with: **illustrative**; **illustration**.

4. Incorporate in sentences:
   (*a*) The **luster** of his act was dimmed by . . .
   (*b*) . . . lost the **luster** . . .

5. Write two synonyms for **lucid.**

Adjectives Ending in *ious*

abstemious   Sparing in diet; refraining from the free use of food and strong drinks; temperate; moderate. (Be sure to have the second syllable, **ste**, rhyme with **key: ab stee′ mi us.**)

Read aloud: He attributed his long life to his **abstemious** use of strong liquor.

The successful man is, as a rule, **abstemious** in his habits.

copious   Plentiful; abundant; full of thought, matter, or the like; profuse in words or style.

Read aloud: You will find a **copious** supply of material in the office.

He possesses a **copious** vocabulary.

His style was too **copious** to be captivating.

The adverb, **copiously**:

Read aloud: Blood flowed **copiously** from the wound.

odious   Deserving or provoking hatred or repugnance; hateful; very displeasing; offensive. (The first syllable is long, as in **go: o′ di us.**)

Read aloud: The people were tired of such **odious** propaganda.

Such **odious** remarks were unmerited.

The stage is no place for **odious** language.

Practice

1. What is the noun form of **odious?**

2. Write two synonyms for **copious.**

3. Construct sentences with: **abstain; refrain** (*v.*).

Verbs Ending in *ize*

extemporize To do, make, or utter on the spur of the moment; to prepare on short notice or from
scanty or unsuitable materials; to speak without special preparation.

Read aloud: He **extemporized** in the absence of the guest
speaker.

She **extemporized** on the benefits of a large vocabulary.

pulverize To reduce to very small particles; to destroy, as
by smashing into fragments; to disintegrate.

Read aloud: We **pulverized** every attempt he made to discredit the work of the mayor.

Yale virtually **pulverized** her opponents in the last game.

galvanize To stimulate or excite as if by an electric shock.

Read aloud: The presence of their old general **galvanized**
them into action.

His talk **galvanized** the members of the football squad.

ostracize To banish from society; to cast out from social
or political favor or fellowship.

Read aloud: The criminal was **ostracized** from society.

All who disagreed with Mr. Swain were **ostracized** from his
circle.

revolutionize To change fundamentally; to produce very great
change in.

Read aloud: The invention of the automobile and airship has
revolutionized travel.

The new executive **revolutionized** the work of the factory.

Increased economy, speed, and power in the automobile and
truck have **revolutionized** transportation.

27

Words for Your Vocabulary

sensible   Having good sense; wise; aware; conscious; perceptibly large.

Read aloud: All acted in a **sensible** way.

He was not **sensible** of my presence.

There is a **sensible** difference in the mentality of the two boys.

dissolve   To separate into component parts; to make liquid; to destroy; to merge entirely; to bring an end to.

Read aloud: The lump of sugar **dissolved** in water.

The audience was **dissolved** in tears during the play.

The leader immediately **dissolved** the assembly.

The noun, **dissolution:**

Read aloud: **Dissolution** of the body takes place after death.

There was a **dissolution** of our firm last year.

odium   Hatred; dislike; reproach; state of being hated; the stigma attaching to what is hateful.

(It is pronounced **o′ di um.**)

Read aloud: He could not wipe out the **odium** of his act.

Those bitter remarks brought **odium** upon him.

She paraded the **odium** of my deed before my friends.

The adjective, **odious:**

Read aloud: The country was teeming with **odious** propaganda.

He made himself **odious** to his subjects.

Practice

1. Use in sentences: **resolve; sensitive.**

2. How does **odium** differ from **hatred?**

Self-Check No. Three

Matching Exercise

Select from Columns II and III a definition of each word in Column I.

I	II	III
1. abstemious	*Adjectives:*	*Verbs:*
2. aggravate	*a.* childish	*k.* annoy
3. copious	*b.* deserved	*l.* blot out
4. credence	*c.* economical	*m.* excite anger of
5. exasperate	*d.* foolish	*n.* improvise
6. extemporize	*e.* fundamental	*o.* make worse
7. fatuous	*f.* hateful	*p.* rebound
8. merited	*g.* obstinate	*Nouns:*
9. obliterate	*h.* overweight	*q.* belief
10. odious	*i.* plentiful	*r.* dishonesty
11. puerile	*j.* temperate	*s.* forcefulness
12. radical		*t.* position of affairs
13. refractory		
14. status		
15. vehemence		

General Exercise

1. Write three synonyms for **obstinate.**

2. Have each adjective modify two nouns: **merited; cardinal; radical.**

3. How does **aggravate** differ in meaning from **exasperate?**

4. Write two synonyms for: **copious; illustrious.**

5. To which syllable of each of the following words must we pay close attention in order to pronounce the word correctly?

credence   puerile   clandestine

44

28

Words Often Confused

laudable	Worthy of being praised; commendable.
laudatory	Pertaining to praise; expressing praise; eulogizing.

(The salient difference between these two words is that the first pertains to receiving praise; the second, to the giving of praise.)

Read aloud: Though he failed, his motives were **laudable**.

To construct so many playgrounds for the children was surely a **laudable** undertaking.

It was difficult for the hero to listen to so many **laudatory** speeches.

What he accomplished was written in **laudatory** verses.

flounder	To plunge about; to struggle without making much progress; to toss; to roll.
founder	To fall in or down; to stumble; to fill with water and sink; to fail.

(We often see these words used in relation to vessels. The first word means that the ship is being tossed about *aimlessly,* perhaps owing to an imperfection in the steering apparatus. The second word refers to a leak and a gradual sinking of the ship.)

Read aloud: The speaker **floundered** so much that the audience became restless.

A **floundering** ship during a heavy fog is a great hazard.

Make a study of words so that you will not **flounder** among outworn expressions.

The vessel **foundered** in the storm.

Practice

1. Write sentences with: **laud; laudation.**

2. Does the same distinction exist between **contemptuous** and **contemptible** as between **laudatory** and **laudable**?

29

Related Words *(confirm)*

confirm   To establish; to strengthen; to render certain; to ratify.
Read aloud: A telegram **confirmed** the order we received yesterday.
The Senate refused to **confirm** the treaty.
What I heard today **confirms** the high opinion I have always had of him.

confirmation   Act of strengthening, ratifying, or sanctioning.
Read aloud: There has been no **confirmation** of his appointment.
Has there been any **confirmation** of his story?

confirmatory   Serving to confirm; corroborative.
Read aloud: We have a letter **confirmatory** to the order.
I received a **confirmatory** look from my employer.

confirmed   Made firm; established; settled by long continuance; habitual.
Read aloud: Brown is a **confirmed** bachelor.
We returned home **confirmed** in our belief that he would make an ideal leader.
He has a **confirmed** dislike for athletics.

Practice

1. Give three synonyms for **confirm.**

2. Use in sentences: **confirmation; conformation.**

3. Construct sentences with: **confirmed dislike; confirmed smoker.**

4. What are the four adjectival forms of **confirm?**

30

Adjectives

vital   Full of life; necessary for life; energetic; full of vigor; fundamentally affecting.

Read aloud: This question is of **vital** importance.

The heart is a **vital** organ.

He played a **vital** part in the last election.

Use in sentences: **vital wound; vital necessity; vital error; vital function.**

salient   Prominent; conspicuous; standing out; easily seen.

(Be sure to give this word three syllables: **sa' li ent. The sa** rhymes with **pay.** It is not pronounced **sal' yent.**)

Read aloud: What is your **salient** objection to my plan?

These were the **salient** points of his speech.

He who occupies a **salient** position must be careful of what he says.

Use in sentences: **salient importance; salient traits; salient features; salient weakness.**

servile   Pertaining to slaves; held in subjection; base; befitting a servant.

(There are two sanctioned pronunciations for this word—the American and the British. In the former, the last syllable **vile** rhymes with **pill;** in the latter, it rhymes with **pile.**)

Read aloud: There were many **servile** revolts before the Civil War.

Some politicians are just the **servile** followers of those in high power.

You may escape **servile** labor by continuing your education.

Practice

1. What are the noun forms of: **vital; servile?**

2. Use in sentences: **vitalize; devitalize.**

47

31

Adjectives Ending in *able*

Here is a simple rule that may strengthen your spelling of this type of word: If the noun form of the word ends in **ation,** the suffix will be **able** and not **ible.** This rule does not cover all **able** words.

Example:	appreciation	appreciable
	calculation	calculable

implacable   Not to be appeased; incapable of being pacified or appeased.

(This word may be pronounced correctly in two ways: **implay′ ka ble** and **implak′ a ble.** The second syllable may be **pla** to rhyme with **slay** or **plac** to rhyme with **crack.**)

Read aloud: The employer was in an **implacable** mood.

He proved an **implacable** foe.

impregnable   Not to be taken by force; able to resist attack; unconquerable.

Read aloud: The fort proved to be **impregnable.**

It was an **impregnable** argument that the attorney presented.

The honesty of our mayor is **impregnable.**

innumerable   Too many to be numbered; very many; numberless.

Read aloud: His acts of kindness were **innumerable.**

I have asked him that question on **innumerable** occasions.

The wants and demands of some people are **innumerable.**

Practice

1. Construct sentences with: **numeral; numerous; enumeration.**

2. Give the noun form of: **placable; numeral.**

48

32

Words for Your Vocabulary

disseminate   To scatter like seed; to spread abroad; to diffuse.
Read aloud: The news of the disaster was quickly **disseminated** throughout the country.
The man was arrested for **disseminating** obscene literature.

corroborate   To make more certain; to confirm.
(It is pronounced **ko rob' o rate.**)
Read aloud: His story was **corroborated** by his brother.
His emaciated face **corroborated** what we heard about his riotous living.

emanate   To go out from; to issue from; to give forth as a flow of light.
Read aloud: The report **emanated** from his enemies.
Happiness **emanated** from his face.

fluctuate   To move like waves; to rise and fall; to waver; to change continually.
Read aloud: Food prices have **fluctuated** during the past year.
Our hopes of victory **fluctuated** from day to day.
We remember how the stock market **fluctuated** in 1930.

evince   To show in a clear manner; to make evident or manifest; to display.
(Accent the last syllable: **evince'.**)
Read aloud: The boy did not **evince** an interest in mathematics.
The child **evinced** great affection for his brother.

Practice

1. Write two synonyms for: **disseminate**; **corroborate**.

2. Consult your dictionary for the derivation of **disseminate**.

33

Pronunciation

amicable (am' icable)
Friendly; peaceable.

This is another word of the difficult **ic** family. The general rule is to accent the syllable that precedes the **ic** syllable, if pronounced **ick**. This word is no exception—the first and not the second syllable is accented.

> *Read aloud:* There was an **amicable** settlement.
> **Amicable** relations exist between the two countries.

bade (băd)
This is the past tense of the verb **bid,** which means *to order; to declare; etc.* It should rhyme with **glad** and not with **aid.**

> *Read aloud:* The officer **bade** the crowd to disperse.
> He **bade** me the time of day and then departed.

irreparable (irrep' arable)
Incapable of being repaired, recovered, or remedied; irretrievable.

To pronounce this word correctly you must accent the second syllable. Do not say **irrepar' able.**

> *Read aloud:* The storm did **irreparable** damage to the crops.
> Her son's death was an **irreparable** loss.
> An **irreparable** breach exists between those two families.
> *Use in sentences:* irreparable injury; irreparable mistake; irreparable wound; irreparable defeat; irreparably upset.

Practice

Does **amicable** denote great warmth of feeling or affection?

34

Words for Your Vocabulary

subterfuge   A trick, excuse, or device used to escape something unpleasant; a place to which one resorts for escape or concealment.

(Pronounce it: **sub′ ter fuj.** The last syllable is the same as the second syllable in **refuge.**)

Read aloud: As a **subterfuge** to go to the ball game, he said that his cousin was dead.

The stomach-ache was only a **subterfuge** to avoid going to school.

By mean **subterfuges** they tried to defeat him for political office.

habituate   To accustom; to familiarize.

(The last syllable of this word, **ate,** must rhyme with **gate.**)

Read aloud: From early youth he became **habituated** to hard work.

She has become so **habituated** to pain that she rarely complains of her suffering.

sanction   To make valid or binding; to approve; to allow.
(*v. and n.*)   (As a noun it means *permission with authority; approval; support.*)

Read aloud: The city lawmakers have **sanctioned** Sunday baseball playing.

His parents did not **sanction** his taking the automobile without their consent.

He received the **sanction** of his employer to go on the political stump.

permeate   To spread through; to pervade; to penetrate; to diffuse itself through.

(This word has three syllables.)

Read aloud: The rain **permeated** the ground.

A feeling of unrest **permeated** the country.

Practice

1. Have **habitual** modify two nouns.

2. Write two synonyms for: **sanction; permeate.**

35

Meaningful Expressions

This section aims to be another reminder that a sure way to embellish your written or oral work is to employ worthwhile adjectival and adverbial expressions. This must not be interpreted to mean that one must use strange or uncommon words. In fact, the opposite is nearer the truth, namely, one should intersperse throughout his conversation harmonious and meaningful expressions made up of appropriate word combinations.

You will note that in many of the illustrations given below, the adjectives and adverbs are simple but at the same time forceful.

A more flexible and colorful speech will accrue to you if you will study and read aloud the sentences containing the phrases and then endeavor to use the same phrases in original sentences. In this way you will gradually make them part of your own vocabulary.

crumbling hopes
crumbling fortune
> *Read aloud:* Lincoln tried hard to bolster the **crumbling hopes** of his army and people.
> His **crumbling fortune** is the result of his wasteful spending.

leaping ambition
leaping flames
> *Read aloud:* The **leaping ambition** of dictators usually precipitates their downfall.
> The firemen battled courageously to prevent the **leaping flames** from damaging the adjoining building.

faltering courage
faltering step
> *Read aloud:* As the hour for the trial appeared, his **faltering courage** dissolved.
> His **faltering step** told us that he had approached the evening of life.

Practice

1. Use in sentences the verb form of: **faltering; crumbling.**

2. How does the word **crumble** differ from **crumple**?

Words for Your Vocabulary

defunct (*adj.*)   Dead; extinct; having finished the course of life or existence.

(This word may also be used as a noun, in which case it means *a dead person*.)

Read aloud: Latin is a **defunct** language.

He invested his money in a magazine which is now **defunct**.

The **defunct** manufacturer left millions to charity.

instigate   To urge forward; to provoke; to incite; to stir up.

Read aloud: The reading of cheap novels **instigated** him to commit the crime.

Who **instigated** the quarrel between the two brothers?

Such libelous talk may **instigate** a lawsuit.

temerity   Rashness; reckless boldness; unreasonable contempt of danger.

(Do not confuse this word with **timidity**, which means *fear*. It is the direct opposite.)

Read aloud: He had the **temerity** to demand a raise in salary during the depression.

To attack an army four times as large as their own was indeed **temerity**.

fallible   Liable to err; liable to be deceived; inaccurate.

(The first syllable in this word rhymes with **gal** in **gallon**.)

Read aloud: All men are **fallible**.

The rumor that we were to go to war proved **fallible**.

Practice

1. Construct three phrases with **defunct**.

2. Use in sentences: **instigation**; **fallacious**.

Self-Check No. Four

Completion Exercise

Complete in the parentheses the right form of the word to be used:

1. He was obliged to perform (serv_____) work.
2. The prices of good meat (fluct_____) during the year.
3. He made many (laud_____) allusions to what we had done.
4. This question is of (vit_____) importance.
5. He has become (habit_____) to suffering.
6. This was his (sali_____) objection to the project.
7. He made a (laud_____) attempt to rescue the child.
8. We have not received a letter (confirm_____) to the order.
9. If you have a large vocabulary, you will not (_____ounder) when called upon to speak.
10. The news of his death was quickly (dissem_____).
11. He refused to (corrob_____) my statement.
12. From what quarters did that story (eman_____)?
13. Damage of an (irrep_____) nature was done to the paintings.
14. A feeling of confidence now (per_____) the country.
15. Will the mayor (sanc_____) this policy?

General Exercise

1. What is the meaning of **instigate?**
2. Use in sentences: **defunct; impregnable.**
3. Have each adjective modify two nouns: **faltering; fallible.**
4. Construct sentences with the noun form of: **confirm; vital.**
5. Define the word **salient.**

37

Words Often Confused

historic   Associated with, or famous in, history.
historical   Pertaining to, or of the nature of, history.
    Read aloud: The recent fight in Congress will prove a **historic** event.
    This book is **historically** true.
    Northwest Passage is a **historical** narrative.

human   Belonging or relating to man; characteristic of man.
humane   Kind; not cruel or beastly.
    Read aloud: Man belongs to the **human** race.
    To err is **human**; to forgive, divine.
    The slaves were treated **humanely** by their master.
    Kindness to dumb animals is the chief teaching of the **Humane** Society.

plausible   Superficially fair, reasonable, or valuable; apparently trustworthy.
feasible   Capable of being done or executed; possible of realization.
    (The fundamental difference between these words seems to be that, while doubt in regard to execution exists in **plausible,** there is the capability or sureness of achievement in **feasible.**)
    Read aloud: His excuse for tardiness was a **plausible** one.
    He presented a **feasible** plan for a new subway.
    The politician offered a **plausible** remedy for our present ills.
    To send a rocket to the moon does not seem **feasible**.

Practice

Give the noun form of: **human**; **humane**; **feasible.**

38

Related Words *(valid)*

valid   Founded on truth or fact; sound; efficient; hav-
       ing force.
  Read aloud: He presented a **valid** argument against retain-
    ing Smith in office.
  The document was found to be **valid**.

validate   To give legal force to; to confirm; to substantiate.
  Read aloud: They refused to **validate** my election.
  Your signature is necessary to **validate** the check.

validity   Truth; soundness; justice; holding good.
  Read aloud: The **validity** of their marriage was established.
  They questioned the **validity** of my argument.

validation   Act of validating; a declaration of validity.
  Read aloud: They are seeking a **validation** of the treaty.

invalid *(adj.)* Without force; without value.
       (The accent is on the second syllable: **in val' id**.)
  Read aloud: The absence of witnesses made the will **invalid**
  The decision of the lower court was considered **invalid**.

invalidate   To weaken or lessen the force of; to destroy the
       authority of; to overthrow.
  Read aloud: His failure to live up to the terms of the agree-
    ment **invalidated** it.
  The absence of two signatures **invalidated** the contract.

Practice

1. Construct sentences with: **valid excuse; valid statement; valid agreement.**

2. What are the roots of: **valor; valid?**

Adjectives

tentative   Done as a trial or experiment; testing; experi-
mental; offered or undertaken provisionally.
(The accent is on the first syllable: **ten' ta tive.**)
Read aloud: **Tentative** arrangements have been made for
his visit to this city.
He submitted a **tentative** plan for saving money for the city.
Use in sentences: **tentative** proposition; **tentative** theory;
tentative arrangement; **tentative** data.

nefarious   Very wicked; infamous; iniquitous.
(The **a** is long, as in **bay: ne fay' ri us.**)
Read aloud: He was sent to jail for his **nefarious** conduct.
The mutilation of the church property was the **nefarious**
work of young men.
Use in sentences: **nefarious** statement; **nefarious** act;
nefarious undertaking; **nefarious** motive.

drastic   Acting with violence or harshness; extreme or rad-
ical in effect; rigorous.
Read aloud: **Drastic** measures were adopted to reduce taxes.
There have been **drastic** changes at the factory this year.
Use in sentences: **drastic** reduction; **drastic** orders; **drastic**
speech; **drastic** cut.

virulent   Extremely poisonous or venomous; bitter in en-
mity; malignant.
(The second syllable, **u,** may have two correct
sounds: like the **u** in **unite,** or like the **oo** in
foot—vir' u lent or **vir' oo lent.** The **i** is
like the **i** in **hit.** This word has no connection
with **virile,** which means *manly, masterful, etc.*)
Read aloud: The doctors found it difficult to check the **virulent**
disease.
His **virulent** pen never seemed to rest.
There was no occasion for his **virulent** attack upon me.

The noun, **virulence:**
Read aloud: There was much **virulence** manifested by the op-
posing party.
The campaign was conducted without **virulence.**

Practice

Illustrate the meaning of: **tenet; tentacle; tenable; tenacious.**

40

Adjectives Ending in *able*

admirable   Excellent; arousing admiration; deserving the highest esteem.

(This word has only one pronunciation. The accent is placed on the *first*, not the *second*, syllable: **ad′ mi ra ble**, never **ad mire′ able**.)

Read aloud: He is a man of **admirable** traits.

The case was handled in an **admirable** way.

They treated us with **admirable** hospitality.

inflammable   Capable of being set on fire; easily enkindled; excitable; irascible; easily provoked.

(The second syllable should rhyme with **jam** and not with **blame**: **in flam′ able**.)

Read aloud: All **inflammable** material was removed from the warehouse.

His **inflammable** disposition got him into much trouble.

The speech aroused the people to an **inflammable** mood.

imperturbable   Incapable of being disturbed or discontented; calm; serene.

Read aloud: Though the enemy was near, the people remained **imperturbable**.

To be **imperturbable** in the face of danger is a fine trait.

interminable   Endless; admitting no limit; boundless; wearisomely protracted.

Read aloud: He is a man of **interminable** wealth.

His generosity is as **interminable** as space.

We were forced to listen to an **interminable** speech.

Practice

1. Does any difference in meaning exist between **flammable** and **inflammable**?

2. Write sentences with: **perturb**; **terminate**.

41

Words for Your Vocabulary

vitalize　　　To endow with life; to animate.
(The first syllable of this word should rhyme with **pie**.)
Read aloud: The teacher found it difficult to **vitalize** her work during the warm spell.
Means were sought to **vitalize** the patriotism of the people.

devitalize　　　To deprive of life or power; to make lifeless.
Read aloud: Fear of defeat **devitalized** their enthusiasm.
Some coaches say that such changes would **devitalize** football.
Such legislation will **devitalize** Congress.

revivify　　　To cause to revive; to reanimate; to reinvigorate.
Read aloud: The colleges are trying to **revivify** interest in interclass sports.
Attempts are being made to **revivify** bicycle riding.

rectify　　　To make or set right; to correct from a wrong or false state; to amend.
Read aloud: The company has agreed to **rectify** the mistake on the bill.
To **rectify** his conscience, he made a complete confession.

Practice

1. Use in sentences: **vital; vitality; vivacity; vivacious.**

2. Give two synonyms for **rectify.**

42

Pronunciation

remedial   (remee′ dial)
Affording a remedy, helping, relieving.

Let the second syllable rhyme with **glee** and not with **lid,** and your pronunciation of this word will be correct.

> *Read aloud:* The lesson was of a **remedial** nature.
>> **Remedial** measures will be taken to improve our vocabulary.
>> **Remedial** reading may be aimed at increasing the eye-span or at quickening the eye movements.

autopsy   (au′ topsy)

This word, whose meaning is known by all, is frequently mispronounced as the result of a misplaced accent. The first and not the second syllable should be accented.

> *Read aloud:* An **autopsy** was performed to learn whether or not the victim had been poisoned.
>> The **autopsy** revealed no foul play.

poinsettia   (poinset′ ti a)

The name of this flower, which is conspicuous during the Christmas season, is often mispronounced as having only three syllables. There are four syllables in this word: **poin set′ ti a.**

> *Read aloud:* The stage was decorated with **poinsettias.**

Practice

1. Construct sentences with: creditable; **remediable.**

2. What letter in **poinsettia** is frequently neglected?

3. How does **remedial** differ from **remediable?**

43

Adjectives

sanguine   Ruddy color; warm; ardent; disposed to be hopeful; confident.

(It is pronounced **sang′ gwin**.)

Read aloud: He has a **sanguine** temperament.

They are living in **sanguine** hopes that rain will soon fall.

The soldiers were **sanguine** of success.

scurrilous   Using language of low indecency; coarsely joking; abusive in an indecent way.

(It is pronounced **skur′ i lus**. The first syllable rhymes with **blur**.)

Read aloud: We refused to read such **scurrilous** literature.

The language used by the young people was **scurrilous**.

Use in sentences: **scurrilous** article; **scurrilous** remarks; **scurrilous** expression; **scurrilous** talk.

habitual   Done by habit; customarily doing a certain thing; used in the practice of a habit; usual; customary.

Read aloud: He is a **habitual** smoker.

Their **habitual** request was for money.

His kindness is **habitual**.

Use in sentences: **habitual** laziness; **habitual** drinker; **habitual** topic; **habitual** nuisance.

Practice

1. What is the verb form of **habitual**? Use it in two different sentences.

2. Use in sentences the following synonyms for **scurrilous**: offensive; opprobrious; vulgar.

3. How many correct pronunciations has **adjectival**?

44

Meaningful Expressions

harrowing tale
harrowing grief

> (**harrowing**: Grievously distressing; heart-rend
> ing; acutely painful.)

Read aloud: He told a **harrowing tale** about the sufferings of the poor.

Her grief is so **harrowing** that she feels she will never again be happy.

gnawing thought
gnawing hunger

Read aloud: He seemed unable to divorce himself from the **gnawing thought** of failure.

Gnawing hunger soon compelled the runaway lad to return home.

demoralizing effect
demoralizing pleasures

Read aloud: Drink had a **demoralizing effect** upon his character.

The wise man will try to avoid the **demoralizing pleasures** of some of our wealthy people.

arbitrarily submitted
arbitrarily imposed

> (**arbitrarily**: In a decisive or despotic way, to
> suit one's own wish or will.)

Read aloud: The **arbitrarily submitted** plan was rejected by the council.

The Colonists were aroused because of the **arbitrarily imposed** taxes of George III.

Practice

Use in sentences: **gnaw; harrow; demoralize; arbitrate**

Words for Your Vocabulary

negligible   That which may be neglected or disregarded; so
small or unimportant that one may disregard
it.
(Accent the first syllable of this word and pronounce it as though it were spelled: **neg′ li ji
ble.**)
Read aloud: There is only a **negligible** difference between
those words.
The damage caused by the fire was **negligible.**
Use in sentences: **negligible price; negligible offense; negligible harm; negligible victory.**

provocative   Tending to provoke, excite, stimulate, or increase
(The accent is placed on the second syllable:
provoc′ ative.)
Read aloud: His facial expression was **provocative** of laugh-
ter.
The trip through the jungle was **provocative** of danger.

erudition   Learning; scholarship; learning in literature, history, or criticism as distinct from the sciences.
(Pronounce this word as though it were spelled
er oo dish′ un. The second syllable, **u,** has
the sound of the **oo** in **foot.**)
Read aloud: He is a man of great **erudition.**
John has a taste for classical **erudition.**

Practice

1.   Show the difference in meaning between **neglectful** and
negligible.

2.   Use the adjective form of **erudition** in a sentence.

3.   Illustrate the meaning of: **provoke; evoke.**

Self-Check No. Five

Matching Exercise

Find in Column II a definition for each word in Column I:

I   II

Adjectives:

     a. capable of being disregarded
     b. capable of being done
1. admirable   *c.* confident
2. sanguine   *d.* deserving highest esteem
3. drastic   *e.* done as an experiment
4. feasible   *f.* done by habit
5. habitual   *g.* endless
6. interminable   *h.* extreme in effect
7. invalid   *i.* favorable
8. nefarious   *j.* reasonable
9. negligible   *k.* tending to excite
10. plausible   *l.* useless
11. provocative   *m.* very wicked
12. rectify   *n.* without effect
13. revivify   *Verbs:*
14. tentative   *o.* affirm with confidence
15. vitalize   *p.* cause to revive
     q. endow with life
     r. make right
     s. turn aside

General Exercise

1. How does **historic** differ from **historical**?

2. Has **flammable** the same meaning as **inflammable**?

3. What is the root word of **vitalize**?

4. Construct sentences with: **negligible**; **tentative**.

5. Have each adjective modify two nouns: **habitual**; **demoralizing**.

6. Write sentences with: **valid**; **invalidate**.

7. Pronounce: **autopsy**; **remedial**; **poinsettia**.

8. Use in sentences the adjectives **human** and **humane**.

9. Use in sentences: **termination**; **provoke**.

10. Pronounce: **invalidate**; **nefarious**; **tentative**; **provocative**.

Words Often Confused

biannual	Occurring twice a year.
biennial	Happening or taking place once in two years.

(Be careful of these words. The members of one or two state legislatures have been forced to blush because of their inaccurate selection of these words. **Bimonthly** means *every two months;* **biweekly** means *every two weeks or semiweekly.* **Biannual** seems to throw the average person on the wrong path.)

Read aloud: Our taxes may be paid **biannually.**

The city elections are held **biennially.**

The **biannual** report will be read at the next meeting.

The **biennial** meeting of the governors effected much good for the unemployed.

beneficent	Doing good; performing acts of charity and kindness.
beneficial	Profitable; helpful; advantageous.

(Some persons, in addition to confusing the use of these words, occasionally mispronounce them. The first word is accented on the second syllable: **benef' icent**; the second is accented on the third syllable: **benefi' cial.**)

Read aloud: The nurse performed many **beneficent** acts for the poor.

This climate will prove **beneficial** to your sickness.

Such constructive criticism should prove **beneficial.**

Practice

1. Consult your dictionary for the meaning of: **biweekly; bimonthly.**

2. Construct sentences with: **beneficence; benefactor.**

3. Write three words not already used on this page which contain the prefix **bene.**

47

Words for Your Vocabulary

explicit   Clearly expressed; outspoken; distinctly stated; having no disguised meaning.
(This word must be accented on the second syllable, not on the first syllable: **expli' cit**.)
Read aloud: The instructions we received were **explicit.**
I wish you would be more **explicit,** as I do not know to what you are referring.
He **explicitly** stated that we were to meet him in this city.

attest   To bear witness to; to certify; to give proof of; to manifest; to affirm to be true or genuine.
(This word must be accented on the last syllable: **attest'**.)
Read aloud: The victory **attested** the splendid type of coaching the team had received.
Did the expert **attest** to the genuineness of the document?
The opening of many factories **attests** to the gradual return to prosperity.

tolerant   Willing to let other people do as they think best; indulgent; willing to endure belief and actions in which one does not partake.
Read aloud: We should be **tolerant** of the religious beliefs of others.
The **tolerant** spirit of the Colonists was taxed to the utmost.
Use in sentences: **tolerant attitude; tolerant look; tolerant audience; tolerant ruler.**

Practice

1. In how many ways may you pronounce the adjective **implicit?**

2. Use in sentences: **tolerable; attestation.**

3. What is the verb form of **tolerant?**

Adjectives

funereal
Of or like a funeral; gloomy; dismal; mournful; sad and solemn.

(This word has four syllables: **fu neer' e al**.)

Read aloud: He has taken a **funereal** outlook upon life.

He always seems to have a **funereal** expression on his face.

Use in sentences: funereal language; funereal atmosphere; funereal silence; funereal gathering.

signal (*adj.*)
Noticeable; distinguished from what is ordinary; remarkable; striking.

Read aloud: His last undertaking was a **signal** success.

What he had to say was of **signal** importance.

Use in sentences: signal failure; signal gesture; signal factor; signal honors.

importunate
Asking repeatedly; troublesomely urgent; persistent; overpressing in request or demand.

(It is pronounced **im por' chu nit**.)

Read aloud: He was an **importunate** child.

They were **importunate** in their requests for better service.

Use in sentences: importunate demands; importunate petitioner; importunate curiosity; importunate requests.

decadent
Falling off; growing worse; declining; deteriorating.

(The accent may be on the second syllable or on the first syllable: **de kay' dent** or **dek' a dent**.)

Read aloud: Do you think Spanish is a **decadent** language?

Bicycle riding, **decadent** for a time, is being revived.

The noun, **decadence** (dekay' dens):

Read aloud: The **decadence** of interest in basketball caused it to be discontinued.

Practice

Construct sentences with: **signalize; opportune.**

Adjectives Ending in *tory*

transitory   Continuing only for a short time; not enduring; fleeting.

Read aloud: Man's stay on earth is **transitory**.

Many young men hazard their lives on the football field just for **transitory** glory.

Earthly pleasures at best are only **transitory**.

commendatory   Pertaining to, or serving for, praise; laudatory. (Do not confuse this word with **commendable**, which means *worthy of being praised*. **Commendatory** signifies *the giving of praise*.)

Read aloud: The official sent a **commendatory** letter to the chief of police for the excellent manner in which he quelled the riot.

It was a **commendatory** speech about our economic administration.

incriminatory   Serving to accuse or charge with a crime or fault.

Read aloud: His testimony was of an **incriminatory** nature.

Many **incriminatory** speeches were heard during the pre-election period.

initiatory   Suitable for an introduction or beginning; introductory; tending to initiate. (This word is pronounced: **ini′ tiato″ ry.** Be sure to give this word six syllables. The second syllable is sounded **nish**, not **nee**.)

Read aloud: His **initiatory** remarks pertained to taxes.

Many members were present at the **initiatory** exercises.

Practice

1. Use in sentences: **commend**; **incriminate**.

2. Illustrate the meaning of: **transient** (*n. and adj.*); **transition**.

50

Words for Your Vocabulary

alternative   Giving or requiring a choice between two things; either of two things or courses offered to one's choice, selection of either one excluding the choice of the other.
(Note that this word pertains to a choice of only two things. It is not good usage to say, "He has the choice of three alternatives." The first syllable, **al,** may be pronounced to rhyme with **pal** or with **fall.**)
Read aloud: The boy received the **alternative** of going to college or learning a trade.
Having to choose between the **alternatives,** war and peace, we selected the latter.

transmit   To send from one person or place to another; to pass something down to one's heirs; to pass along.
(Accent this word on the last syllable: **transmit'.**)
Read aloud: The telephone **transmits** sound to a great distance.
Rats can **transmit** disease.
The teacher ably **transmitted** her thoughts to the class.

lavish (*v.*)   To pour out or spend profusely; to squander; to bestow with profusion.
Read aloud: She **lavished** affection upon the lost child.
The people **lavished** praise upon the mayor for his splendid work.

The adjective, **lavish:** Very abundant; profuse; expending greatly:
Read aloud: He helped himself to a **lavish** serving of cake.
Such **lavish** spending crippled the country.
The administration was criticized for its **lavish** expenditures.

Practice

1. How many pronunciations has the noun **alternate?**

2. Construct sentences with: **transmission; intermittent.**

51

Pronunciation

desultory   (des′ ultory)
   Jumping, or passing, from one thing to another, without order or rational connections; aimless; not connected with the subject.

In this word the primary accent should be on the first syllable, **des,** and not on the second syllable. It is incorrect to say **desul′ tory.**

> *Read aloud:* The careful reading of a few authors is better than the **desultory** reading of many.
> We paid no attention to his **desultory** remarks.

heinous   (hay′ nus)
   Hateful; flagrant; odious; atrocious; giving great offense.

Let the first syllable, **hei,** be pronounced **hay** and not **hee,** and you will encounter no difficulty with this word.

> *Read aloud:* A more **heinous** crime could not be committed.
> Such **heinous** propaganda should not be tolerated.

grimace   (grimace′)
   A distortion of the face whether voluntary or from affection; funny or ugly look.

Accent the last syllable and let it rhyme with **face.** Do not say **grim′ us.**

> *Read aloud:* The comedian's **grimaces** brought forth much laughter.
> His **grimaces** were caused by intense pain.

Practice

1. Give two synonyms for **heinous.**

2. Where is the accent in: **desultory; grimace?**

52

Adjectives Ending in *able*

These are called "borrowed" **able** words, inasmuch as they conform to no particular rule of spelling.

delectable   Very pleasing; delightful.
> *Read aloud:* The members of the party were in a **delectable** mood.
> We had many **delectable** meals at your house.

inscrutable   Incapable of being searched into or understood; unknowable.
>   (It is pronounced **in skroo′ ta ble.** The second syllable should rhyme with **zoo.**)
> *Read aloud:* He spoke of the **inscrutable** wisdom of God.
> His face took on an **inscrutable** expression.

redoubtable   That should be feared or dreaded; formidable.
>   (The pronunciation is **re dout′ a ble.** The second syllable rhymes with **scout.**)
> *Read aloud:* His last victory proved him to be a **redoubtable** leader.
> The opponents presented a **redoubtable** argument.

inexorable   Not to be moved or persuaded by entreaty or prayer; unyielding; relentless.
>   (Note that the second syllable is pronounced **ek,** and not **eg: in ek′ so ra ble.**)
> *Read aloud:* They were **inexorable** in their demands.
> He was an **inexorable** judge.

Practice

Use in sentences: **scrutinize; hospitality.**

53

Meaningful Expressions

inexpressibly happy
inexpressibly powerful

> *Read aloud:* The father is **inexpressibly happy** because his child is recovering from a serious malady.
>
> He was an **inexpressibly powerful** ruler.

opportunely arrived
opportunely planned

> (**opportunely**: In a well-chosen, favorable, or suitable way.)
>
> *Read aloud:* The police **opportunely arrived** at the scene of the trouble.
>
> The meeting of the two leaders was **opportunely planned.**

precarious fortune
precarious course

> (**precarious**: Uncertain; insecure; not safe; characterized by instability. The second syllable **car** rhymes with **dare.**)
>
> *Read aloud:* Stocks and bonds in a period of bankruptcy prove a **precarious** fortune.
>
> We counselled him about the **precarious** course he was taking.

chronic grumbler
chronic complaint

> (**chronic**: Continuing a long time; constant; habitual; confirmed.)
>
> *Read aloud:* A **chronic grumbler** is unwelcome at any gathering.
>
> His **chronic complaint** was that he was underpaid.

Practice

1. Name two synonyms for **inexpressibly.**

2. Use in sentences: **importune; opportunist; expressive; chronological.**

54

Words for Your Vocabulary

phlegmatic Sluggish; indifferent; not easily moved; cool.
(The first syllable is pronounced **fleg**.)
Read aloud: He is very **phlegmatic** with respect to the danger of working in mines.
She has a **phlegmatic** nature which prevents her from being easily excited.

exterminate To destroy completely; to root out; to annihilate.
(Accent the second syllable of this word.)
Read aloud: Attempts have been made to **exterminate** the rats from the city.
St. Patrick is said to have **exterminated** snakes from Ireland.

terminate To put an end to; to end; to form the conclusion of, as a story.
Read aloud: My services with this firm will **terminate** next week.
I did not like the way the story **terminated**.
Words that **terminate** in *atory* are very pleasing to the ear.

blatant Noisy; loud-mouthed; demanding undue attention; coarse.
(The first syllable in this word is pronounced **blay**.)
Read aloud: The country soon tired of the **blatant** reformer.
His **blatant** voice could always be heard above the rest.

Practice

Use in sentences: **terminal; phlegmatically; termination; blatancy.**

Self-Check No. Six

Completion Exercise

beneficent	desultory	redoubtable
blatant	explicit	signal
chronic	inexorable	tolerant
delectable	inexpressible	transitory

Fill each blank with an adjective from the above list. Some adjectives may be used twice. Every adjective must be used at least once.

1.	_____ glory	11.	_____ decree
2.	_____ importance	12.	_____ honors
3.	_____ complaint	13.	_____ bequest
4.	_____ judge	14.	_____ disease
5.	_____ remarks	15.	_____ disposition
6.	_____ voice	16.	_____ meal
7.	_____ speech	17.	_____ grief
8.	_____ instructions	18.	_____ acts
9.	_____ nature	19.	_____ spirit
10.	_____ fortress	20.	_____ crowd

General Exercise

1. Construct sentences with: **transmit; incriminatory.**

2. **Alternation** means a change among how many things?

3. How does **biennial** differ in meaning from **biannual**?

4. What is the sound of the last syllable of **importunate**? Does it rhyme with **gate** or **hit**?

5. What is the verb form of: **signal; importunate?**

6. Use in sentences: **attest; precarious.**

7. Pronounce: **heinous; grimace; blatant.**

8. Have the word **signal** qualify two nouns.

55

Words Often Confused

affect   To pretend or assume; to influence or impress.
effect (*v.*)   To bring to pass; to accomplish.

The use of the last word as a verb causes considerable difficulty. If one will associate with it the idea *to bring about as a result*, he will find it an easy, as well as a very useful, word.

> *Read aloud:* He always **affects** seriousness in the presence of my parents.
> The news of the disaster **affected** the entire country.
> His **affected** (*adj.*) loyalty was easily detected.
> We could not **effect** a treaty with your country.
> Mr. Brown, through his generosity, has **effected** much good among the poor.
> The delegates departed without **effecting** their purpose.

dispassionate   Unprejudiced; free from passion or feeling; calm; impartial.
unimpassioned   Not impassioned; not actuated by passion or zeal; without ardor.

Dispassionate applies to what is uninfluenced by feeling or passion. **Unimpassioned** applies to that which does not itself manifest warmth of feeling.

> *Read aloud:* He was a **dispassionate** commentator, taking the part of neither contesting side.
> A judge should always take a **dispassionate** view of the case.
> We were not impressed by his **unimpassioned** speech.
> The brother of the accused remained an **unimpassioned** spectator throughout the trial.

Practice

1. Has **affect** any connection with **effective?**

2. Use in sentences: **effectuate; affectation.**

3. Select the proper form in the parentheses:

    a. The depression (**affected, effected**) the whole nation.
    b. His speech is bound to (**affect, effect**) much good.
    c. The improvement (**affected, effected**) by these charitable organizations in the slum areas cannot be estimated.
    d. She (**affects, effects**) a Bostonian accent.

56

Synonyms

Try to see the difference in meaning that exists in the following words. It would be well to construct original sentences with each of them.

obscure   Not well known; not clear.
   Read aloud: The poet lives in an **obscure** little town.
   Don't you think his style is somewhat **obscure**?

ambiguous   Having two meanings; doubtful.
   Read aloud: His answer was **ambiguous**.
   We were left in an **ambiguous** position by his failure to appear.

involved   Confused; mixed.
   Read aloud: Our finances are in an **involved** condition.
   His remarks were so **involved** that we paid no attention to them.

abstruse   Hard to understand.
   Read aloud: John found philosophy an **abstruse** subject.
   I dislike having to study so many **abstruse** rules.

unintelligible   That which cannot be understood.
   Read aloud: He gave me an **unintelligible** explanation.
   His English is almost **unintelligible**.

complicated   Hard to understand; made worse.
   Read aloud: His refusal to be present will **complicate** matters.
   He found himself in a **complicated** position.

enigmatical   Puzzling; perplexing; mysterious.
   Read aloud: He is surely an **enigmatical** person.
   Such **enigmatical** testimony was not accepted.

Practice

1. Use in sentences: **obscurity**; **enigma**.

2. Show the difference in meaning between **abstruse** and **abstract**.

3. What is the noun form of: **ambiguous**; **complicated**?

4. Is the word **complex** related to the word **complicated**? Prove your answer.

57

Adjectives

devastating   Destroying; laying waste; making desolate.
Read aloud: It was the most **devastating** fire of the year.
Try to avoid such **devastating** pleasures.
Use in sentences: **devastating work; devastating plague; devastating loss; devastating power.**

inordinate   Unregulated; excessive; lacking order or right arrangement; unrestrained.
(The accent is on the second syllable: **in or′ di nit.**)
Read aloud: He has an **inordinate** love of the classics.
His weight is the result of **inordinate** eating.
All reserves were called out to build a wall against the **inordinate** power of the Ohio in flood.
Use in sentences: **inordinate desires; inordinate drinker; inordinate fear; inordinate anger.**

scathing   Bitterly severe; scorching; wounding severely.
(The **a** is long, as in **fade.**)
Read aloud: He received a **scathing** rebuke for his negligence.
There was a **scathing** editorial on the incompetency of the judge.
Use in sentences: **scathing criticism; scathing reprimand; scathing note; scathing answer.**

atrocious   Savagely brutal; very wicked or cruel.
(Pronounce it: **a trow′ shus.** The second syllable rhymes with **flow.**)
Read aloud: He was electrocuted for his **atrocious** deed.
The prisoners received **atrocious** treatment from the enemy.

Practice

1. Give three synonyms for **scathing.**

2. Use in sentences: **devastate; inordinately.**

Adjectives Ending in *ious*

devious   Out of the direct way; winding; without a fixed course; going astray; erring.
(It is pronounced **dee′ vi us**.)
Read aloud: We took a **devious** route on the way back from the game.
He seems to have a **devious** conscience.
Having plenty of time, we took a **devious** way home.

hilarious   Mirthful; noisy; merry; very gay.
(There are two correct pronunciations for this word: the **i** in the first syllable may be short, as in **pin**, or it may be long, as in **pine**. The second syllable, **lar,** should rhyme with **glare**: **hi lar′ i us**.)
Read aloud: The students were **hilarious** as a result of the great football victory.
It may have been drink that made them so **hilarious**.

The noun, **hilarity**:
Read aloud: The police were called at midnight to put an end to the **hilarity** at the home of my neighbor.

officious   Volunteering one's services where they are neither asked nor needed; meddlesomeness; minding other people's business.
(The pronunciation is **o fish′ us**. The **o** is as in **connect**.)
Read aloud: We soon tired of that **officious** person.
Mr. Crane disliked the **officious** manner of his assistant.

Practice

1. Illustrate in a sentence the meaning of **deviate**.

2. Use the following synonyms for **officious** in sentences: **arbitrary; positive; dictatorial.**

Words for Your Vocabulary

divergent   Different; characterized by disagreement; receding farther and farther from each other.

(The **i** in the first syllable may be long, as in **ice,** or short, as in **pin.** In both cases, the accent must be on the second syllable: **diver′ gent.**)

Read aloud: Their statements were **divergent.**

The two **divergent** lines lead to opposite sides of the lake.

A compromise with those of **divergent** ideas was impossible.

simulate   To pretend; to feign; to counterfeit; to imitate; to have the mere appearance of.

(Do not confuse this word with **stimulate,** which means *to arouse or excite.*)

Read aloud: The students **simulated** interest in the course.

The prisoner **simulated** insanity.

His knowledge of the subject is only **simulated.**

hypothetical   Assumed without proof; supposed; concerned with hypotheses.

(The first syllable may be pronounced **high** or **hip.**)

Read aloud: The reasons he gave for the trouble were **hypothetical.**

He is a **hypothetical** thinker.

Hypothetical questions are sometimes hard to answer.

Practice

1. Use in sentences: **simulate; stimulate.**

2. Construct sentences with: **diverge; hypothesis.**

60

Pronunciation

impotent   (im′ potent)
> Wanting power, strength, or vigor, whether physical or intellectual.

The fact that **potent** is accented on the syllable **po** may be the cause of the mispronunciation of **impotent**. This word must be accented on the first syllable.

> *Read aloud:* He proved to be an **impotent** leader.
> The man stood **impotent** while the robbers ransacked his home.

accompanist   (ac com′ pa nist)
> One who accompanies; a musician who plays an indispensable accompanying part.

Because the verb form of this word is **accompany**, many are led to think that the noun should be spelled with a **y**. This is incorrect. There is no **y** in the word. It has four and not five syllables.

> *Read aloud:* Mr. Jones was the **accompanist**.
> She found it difficult to sing with a piano **accompanist**.

percolator   (pur′ ko la tor)
In pronouncing this word, focus your attention on the vowel in the second syllable, which is **o** and not **u**. Say **per′ co la tor**, not **per′ cu la tor**.

> *Read aloud:* The coffee is in the **percolator**.

Practice

1. Construct sentences with: **potent; potential.**
2. Use in sentences: **percolate; accompanist.**

61

Adjectives

incisive   Cutting; sharp; penetrating; sarcastic; biting. (Pronounce this word **inci′ sive.** The second syllable, **ci,** should rhyme with **fly.**)

Read aloud: He received an **incisive** rebuke from his superior.

She has an **incisive** voice.

Did you read his **incisive** criticism?

The question evoked an **incisive** answer from him.

Use in sentences: **incisive look; incisive editorial; incisive style; incisive wit.**

visionary   Dreamy; imaginative; not practical; not having solid foundation.

Read aloud: He is a **visionary** mortal.

His **visionary** scheme did not appeal to the public.

It proved to be a **visionary** plan.

His is a **visionary** outlook upon life.

Use in sentences: **visionary talk; visionary project; visionary scheme; visionary statement.**

compatible   Able to exist together or get on well together; consistent; in harmony.

Read aloud: These are **compatible** colors.

His words and acts are not **compatible.**

Truth is not **compatible** with falsity.

His spending is not **compatible** with his salary.

Use in sentences: **compatible ideas; compatible remarks; compatible demands; compatible with reason.**

Practice

Give two synonyms for: **visionary; compatible.**

62

Meaningful Expressions

coercive measures
coercive authority
> (coercive: Compelling; tendency to compel by law or authority.)
>
> *Read aloud:* Coercive measures were used to collect back taxes.
>
> The authority of their ruler was coercive.

labored style
labored speech
> *Read aloud:* His labored style detracted from the interest of his work.
>
> The politician's labored speech did not win him many followers.

judicial dignity
judicial glasses
> *Read aloud:* The members of the court maintained a judicial dignity during the nationwide criticism of their act.
>
> I shall try to view this case through judicial glasses.

liquid assets
liquid eloquence
> *Read aloud:* The assets of the bank are now liquid.
>
> Webster's liquid eloquence gave him a national reputation.

intolerably long
intolerably mean
> *Read aloud:* The speech was intolerably long.
>
> He was intolerably mean to his subordinates.

Practice

1. What is the verb form of: coercive; tolerable?

2. Use in sentences: liquefy; coercion.

Words for Your Vocabulary

immortalize To cause to live or exist forever; to endow with everlasting life; to perpetuate in fame.
(Accent the second syllable: **immor' talize.**)
Read aloud: Edison's many inventions will **immortalize** his name.
His glorious deeds are **immortalized** in prose and poetry.

coalesce To unite in one body or product; to combine in one body or community.
(It is pronounced **ko a les'.** The last syllable, **lesce**, rhymes with **guess.**)
Read aloud: The two parties have **coalesced.**
If those clouds **coalesce,** I fear we shall have a severe thunderstorm.

justify To give a good reason for; to show to be just or right; to pronounce free from guilt or blame.
Read aloud: The comparative scarcity of diamonds **justifies** their high price.
He was **justified** in making the complaint.
Was he able to **justify** the stand he took on prohibition?

The adjective, **justifiable:**
Read aloud: That his act was **justifiable** cannot be denied.
Their **justifiable** demands were presented to the manufacturers.

refute To prove a statement, claim, or the like, to be false or incorrect; to disprove and overthrow by argument or proof.
(Accent the last syllable: **refute'.**)
Read aloud: He tried to **refute** the charge that he was driving while under the influence of liquor.
That he has been a success cannot be **refuted.**

Practice

Use in sentences: **justifiable; justification; refutable; refutation.**

Self-Check No. Seven

Completion Exercise

Verbs		Adjectives	
affect	immortalize	ambiguous	inordinate
coalesce	justify	coercive	judicial
coerce	refute	compatible	labored
effect	simulate	devastating	officious
		devious	scathing
		divergent	unintelligible
		hilarious	visionary

Fill each blank with an appropriate word from the above list:

1. That work will _____ his name.
2. The story did not _____ me that way.
3. He did not attempt to _____ my statement.
4. It was easy for her to _____ sympathy.
5. That did not _____ his using such language.
6. We shall try to _____ a reconciliation between the brothers.
7. He possesses a(n) _____ appetite.
8. Did you read the _____ editorial in this morning's paper?
9. His schemes were of a(n) _____ nature.
10. They were _____ as a result of the victory.
11. We returned by a(n) _____ path.
12. That question is very _____.
13. The foreigner's remarks were _____.
14. The flood was _____ to the orange groves.
15. We disliked his _____ manner.

General Exercise

1. Write two synonyms for **obscure**.

2. Use in sentences: **simulate; stimulate**.

3. Have **coercive** modify two nouns.

4. Define **divergent**.

5. Give the verb form of: **devastating; tolerable**.

64

Words Often Confused

complement   Something which completes or fills up; the number required to make something complete. *As a verb,* to supply a lack.

compliment   A form of flattery; an expression of praise.

Complete: The army has filled its _____.

Let me _____ you for your excellent work.

The _____ of an angle of 60° is one of 30°.

Two more acts are needed to _____ the program.

He refused to accept my _____.

ability   The power to do a thing.

capacity   The power of receiving or containing; position.

Complete: He demonstrated his _____ as an actor.

His reading _____ is very great.

The seating _____ of the theater is limited.

Kindly contribute according to your financial _____

He acted in the _____ of chairman.

acceptance   The act of accepting or receiving.

acceptation   The meaning of a word or statement as generally understood.

Complete: That word has a different _____.

His _____ of the gift made him subservient to the giver.

What is the general _____ of the word **acclimate?**

I notified Mr. Erk of my _____ of the position.

What is your _____ of that remark?

Practice

Construct sentences with: **acceptable; supplement; capacious; complimentary.**

85

65

Words for Your Vocabulary

sedentary   Characterized by, or requiring, sitting; staying in one and the same place; that which keeps one sitting a good deal.

(It is pronounced **sed′ en ta″ ry**.)

Read aloud: He should exercise more, because his work is of a **sedentary** nature.

He has refused a bookkeeping position because it was too **sedentary**.

dissertation   An extended treatment of a subject; a formal discussion; an essay; a thesis.

Read aloud: We enjoyed his **dissertation** on the advantages of a college education.

The **dissertation** on the gold standard was entirely too long and too vague.

derision   Scornful laughter; ridicule; state of being mocked.

(This word must be pronounced **de rizh′ un**.)

Read aloud: Fearing the **derision** of the audience, he refused to deliver his speech.

The **derision** of his classmates made him a very sensitive boy.

Derision followed the speaker's remarks.

The adjective, **derisive** (Be sure to pronounce it **de rye′ sive** and not **de ris′ ive**. The second syllable rhymes with **cry** and not with **bliss**.):

Read aloud: The accused man could not escape the **derisive** taunts of the crowd.

His **derisive** remarks penetrated very deeply.

Practice

1. Use in sentences: **deride; risible.**

2. Give two synonyms for **dissertation.**

3. Have **sedentary** modify two nouns.

66

Adjectives

intermittent   Coming and going at intervals; alternating; periodic; recurrent.

(The accent is placed on the third syllable, **mit**.)

Read aloud: There were **intermittent** showers during the day.

The **intermittent** noises at night disturbed my sleep.

The people are clamoring for a lasting and not **intermittent** prosperity.

Profits and losses were **intermittent** during the past year.

Use in sentences: **intermittent** pleasures; **intermittent** fever; **intermittent** sunshine; **intermittent** laughter.

insidious   Full of plots; deceitful; intended to entrap; sly; working secretly.

(Be sure to give four syllables to this word.)

Read aloud: Leprosy is an **insidious** disease.

We refused to listen to such **insidious** propaganda.

He fell a victim to their **insidious** promises.

Use in sentences: **insidious** remark; **insidious** expression; **insidious** motive; **insidious** undertaking.

irresistible   That which cannot be successfully resisted; superior to opposition; resistless; incapable of being withstood.

Read aloud: She has an **irresistible** smile.

The place was an **irresistible** attraction.

It proved to be an **irresistible** fortress.

Use in sentences: **irresistible** offer; **irresistible** temptation.

Practice

1. Write three words that end in **mit**.

2. Explain the meaning of the prefix in: **transmit**; **intermittent**.

3. How does **insidious** differ in meaning from **iniquitous**?

4. Give two words that contain the prefix **ir**.

5. Name three words related to or evolved from **resist**.

6. Write two synonyms for **irresistible**.

Adjectives Ending in *tory*

adulatory
Characterized by, or given to, flattery; giving excessive praise.

(The primary accent is on the first syllable: **ad′ ulato″ ry.**)

Read aloud: It was an **adulatory** address.

The average man is not opposed to receiving **adulatory** comments for his work.

denunciatory
Pertaining to, or characterized by, accusing, threatening, or condemning.

(You may pronounce this word correctly in two ways: as if spelled **de nun′ si a to″ ry** or **de nun′ shi a to″ ry.**)

Read aloud: Such **denunciatory** remarks were unmerited.

His question brought forth a **denunciatory** answer from the professor.

retaliatory
Pertaining to the return of like for like; inflicting in return.

(Be sure to pronounce this word with six syllables.)

Read aloud: As a **retaliatory** measure, the enemy treated our prisoners cruelly.

The Boston Tea Party was a **retaliatory** act on the part of the Colonists.

Practice

1. Construct sentences with the noun forms of: **adulatory;** **retaliatory.**

2. Use in sentences: **denounce; retaliate.**

3. Have **retaliatory** modify two nouns.

4. Give two synonyms for: **adulatory; denunciatory.**

68

Words for Your Vocabulary

ratify   To confirm; to approve; to sanction; to verify.
Read aloud: Congress refused to **ratify** Smith's appointment.
The agreement was not **ratified** by the directors.

The noun, **ratification**:
Read aloud: There was no **ratification** of the treaty by Congress.
A **ratification** of the contract took place at the last meeting.

procrastinate   To put off till later; to waste time when one should act; to delay action through laziness or indecision.
Read aloud: He who **procrastinates** rarely accomplishes his purpose.
She **procrastinated** so much about buying the dress that when she went to purchase it, she found that it had been sold.

The noun, **procrastination**:
Read aloud: His **procrastination** resulted in the loss of his position.

prodigal   Given to reckless extravagance; wasteful; characterized by profuse expenditure.
Read aloud: Poverty was the result of his **prodigal** living.
The people were **prodigal** spenders during the war.

deface   To destroy or mar the face or external appearance of; to spoil or injure by removing important features of.
Read aloud: The children **defaced** the wall with chalk-writing.
He tried to **deface** the note.
That building **defaces** our neighborhood.

Practice

1. Give the noun form of: **ratify; prodigal.**

2. Use in sentences: **defacement; ratifiable.**

69

Pronunciation

municipal   (munis′ ipal)
Having to do with the affairs of the city, town, or nation.

Too frequently, this word is mispronounced **municip′ al.** The accent should be on the second and not on the third syllable.

> *Read aloud:* The letter was referred to the **municipal** authorities.
>
> A celebration was held in the **municipal** building.

comparable   (kom′ parable)
Capable of being compared (with); worthy of comparison (to).

Accent the first syllable, **com,** and not the second. It is incorrect to say **compair′ able.**

> *Read aloud:* Their records are **comparable** in regard to efficiency.
>
> His wealth is **comparable** to that of his brother.

project (*v.*)   (project′)
To throw or cast forward; to cause to protrude; to devise.

As a verb this word must be accented on the last syllable : **project′.**

> *Read aloud:* The rock **projected** far into the water.
>
> He **projected** his plan before the members.
>
> The pictures were **projected** upon the screen.

clique   **cleek** or **click**
A narrow circle of persons associated by common interests; a small and exclusive set.

Dictionaries now record two pronunciations for this word. Formerly it had to be **cleek.**

> *Read aloud:* He belongs to an influential **clique.**
>
> **Cliques** were not tolerated at that institution.

Practice

1. What are the noun forms of: **municipal; comparable?**
2. Use in a sentence the word **incomparably.**

Verbs Ending in *ize*

neutralize   To reduce to inefficiency; to counteract; to render inactive.
Read aloud: Losing his temper **neutralized** the good effect of his speech.
Often one poison is used to **neutralize** another poison.

synchronize   To happen or take place at the same time; to make agree in time.
Read aloud: The clocks in this building do not **synchronize**.
The steps and movements of the two tap dancers **synchronize** perfectly.

tyrannize   To rule with unjust and oppressive severity; to exercise arbitrary power.
Read aloud: He so **tyrannized** over his subjects as to cause a revolution.
The members of the organization refused to be **tyrannized** over.

dogmatize   To make declarations or contend confidently or arrogantly; to speak or write dogmatically or positively.
Read aloud: The preacher **dogmatized** too much to please his congregation.
To **dogmatize** is often a failing of those in high authority.

demoralize   To corrupt or undermine morals or moral principles; to weaken or render untrustworthy in discipline, efficiency, or the like.
Read aloud: Excessive drinking **demoralized** the people.
The last defeat **demoralized** the army.

soliloquize   To talk to oneself; to say or address in a soliloquy.
Read aloud: He **soliloquized** upon the maltreatment he received from his superiors.

Meaningful Expressions

unalloyed pleasures
unalloyed happiness

> *Read aloud:* It seemed that his life was one of **unalloyed pleasures.**
>
> Such **unalloyed happiness** was the fitting end of a good and upright life.

substantial gains
substantial increase

> *Read aloud:* **Substantial gains** in the business world will be a sure sign that the depression has ended.
>
> A **substantial increase** in salary was given to the executive.

supine ruler
supine position

> (**Supine** is accented on the last syllable, which rhymes with **fine: su pine'.** It means: lying flat on the back; listless; indifferent to one's duty or to the needs of others.)
>
> *Read aloud:* The **supine ruler** was responsible for the revolution.
>
> If you lie in a **supine position,** you will rest your entire body.

sprightly conversation
sprightly gait

> (**sprightly:** Lively; brisk; vigorous; gay.)
>
> *Read aloud:* We listened to the **sprightly conversation** of the two young girls.
>
> His **sprightly gait** would make you think that he was twenty years younger than his actual age.

withering beauty
withering look

> *Read aloud:* A realization of her **withering beauty** made her very unhappy.
>
> The students failed to escape the **withering look** of the professor.

Practice

1. Use in sentences the verb forms of: **withering; substantial.**

2. Construct sentences with: **alloy** (*v.*); **allay.**

Words for Your Vocabulary

judicious   Wise; sensible; having, using, or showing good judgment.

Read aloud: His remarks were **judicious** and right to the point.

The appointment of Jones proved to be a **judicious** one.

The antonym, **injudicious**:

Read aloud: It was **injudicious** on his part to break training before the big event.

It would be **injudicious** to increase the taxpayer's burden.

inculcate   To teach and impress by frequent repetitions; to urge on the mind.

(This word may be pronounced correctly in two ways: **in kul′ kate** and **in′ kul kate**.)

Read aloud: "Christ **inculcates** humility on his followers."

The teacher tried to **inculcate** honesty in the minds of the pupils.

imputation   Act of charging or accusing; the attributing of responsibility, authorship, possession, *etc.*

Read aloud: The **imputation** was that he stole the goods from the automobile.

No **imputation** of dishonesty has ever been made against him.

subordinate (*v.*) To place in a lower order or class; to consider of less value or importance; to make dependent on.

Read aloud: He **subordinated** work to pleasure.

They refused to **subordinate** themselves to their employers.

Practice

1. Use in sentences: **judicial**; **subordinate** (*adj.*).

2. What is the verb form of **imputation**?

Self-Check No. Eight

Completion Exercise

Complete the spelling of the proper form of the word in the parentheses:

1. We have just finished a (subs_____) meal.
2. The treaty has not been (rat_____).
3. A successful person does not (procra_____).
4. His wealth is not (comp_____) to ours.
5. The (der_____) of his friends made him uneasy.
6. He does not like (seden_____) work.
7. His appointment was a (judi_____) one.
8. The (imputa_____) was that I was lazy.
9. One should (subo_____) pleasure to business.
10. The moving pictures prove an (irres_____) attraction to most children.
11. We shall not resort to (retali_____) measures.
12. He proved to be a (supi_____) leader.
13. She was (prodi_____) with her money.
14. The children (defac_____) the property.
15. There was (intermit_____) applause throughout his speech.

General Exercise

1. Write two expressions with: **unalloyed; irresistible.**

2. Give an antonym for: **comparable; irreparable.**

3. Pronounce: **derisive; municipal.**

4. Construct sentences with: **neutralize; demoralize.**

5. Illustrate the meaning of: **inculcate; dissertation.**

6. Consult your dictionary for the difference in meaning of **impute** and **ascribe.**

7. Write two synonyms for: **dissertation; insidious.**

8. Is **ridiculous** related in any way to the root of **derision?**

9. How does **adulation** differ from **praise?**

10. What is the adjective form of **dogmatize?**

73

Words Often Confused

allusion   A slight reference to something.
illusion   A mistaken perception; an error of vision.
delusion   A mistaken conviction; an error of the mind.

Complete: A mirage is a(n) —————.
You labor under a(n) ————— if you think vocabulary building is difficult.
No ————— was made to his absence.
His letter contained no ————— to his recent illness.
To think he was superior to his brother was a(n) —————.

vocation   One's real work or profession.
avocation   Some work aside from one's regular work.

Complete: The lawyer followed his —————, which was painting, with enthusiasm.
Teaching golf in the summer was the doctor's —————.
Every man should devote much time and energy to his —————.
In the evening he studied art as a(n) —————.
One could readily see that his ————— was medicine.
I believe one should have some ————— that is radically different from his profession.

majority   More than half the whole number.
plurality   More votes than the next highest candidate received; the excess of votes of one candidate over another.

Complete: Jones received 20 votes, Burns 15 votes, and Smith 3 votes; Jones's ————— was only one vote.
Burns's ————— over Smith was 12 votes.
A ————— of 60 people must be a number that is in excess of 30.
Usually there must be a ————— to constitute a quorum.

Practice

1. Illustrate the meaning of: **delude; allude; elude.**
2. Construct sentences with: **elusive; delusive.**

74

Words with the Prefix *bene*

Our language is well equipped with words that contain the prefix **bene,** which means *well.* To be able to incorporate them in your written or oral speech will surely improve it.

benevolent   Having a disposition to do good; charitable; kindly; wishing well.

                     (Pronounce it **be nev′ o lent.** The first **e** is like the first **e** in **event.**)

Read aloud: His **benevolent** acts are known throughout the country.

He was great because of his **benevolent** disposition.

benevolence   Good will; kindly feeling; act of kindness.

Read aloud: Humanity has shared in the **benevolences** of Pasteur.

He came to seek another **benevolence.**

benefaction   A charitable donation; a kind act; help given for any good purpose.

                     (The primary accent should be placed on the third syllable: **ben e fac′ tion.**)

Read aloud: Nature showered **benefactions** on him.

His latest **benefaction** was the building of a playground for the poor.

benediction   An expression of blessing, prayer, or kind wishes.

Read aloud: The soldier received his parents' **benediction** before departing for the front.

Well-run banks continued along the old lines, with the **benediction** of the administration.

Practice

Construct sentences with: **benefactor; beneficent.**

75

Adjectives

voracious   Greedy in eating; ravenous; excessively eager; immoderate.
Read aloud: He is a **voracious** eater.
A more **voracious** reader could not be found.
Such a **voracious** appetite is expensive to its owner.
He was a **voracious** worker.
Use in sentences: **voracious** child; **voracious** politician; **voracious** crowd; **voracious** animal.

callous   Hardened; unfeeling.
Read aloud: He was **callous** to the ridicule of his enemies.
The **callous** youth manifested no regret for his act.

impetuous   Rushing with force and violence; vehement in feeling; acting hastily, rashly, or with sudden feeling.
Read aloud: The stream was **impetuous** after the heavy rainfall.
The boy repented his **impetuous** step.
His **impetuous** temper blinded him to the real wants of his people.
He rushed **impetuously** at his older brother.

dexterous   Ready and expert in the use of the body and limbs; skillful with the hands; quick at inventing expedients; skillful; artful.
Read aloud: It shows **dexterous** workmanship.
An artist must be **dexterous** in his work.
The golfer hit the ball with a **dexterous** hand.

Practice

1. Pronounce: **despicable; applicable.**
2. Construct sentences with: **dexterity; voracity.**

76

Adjectives Ending in *lent*

Let us try some words that end in **lent** or **ulent**, which means *full of.*

opulent   Wealthy; rich; abundant; profuse; plentiful; lavish.
    Read aloud: That family is now in **opulent** circumstances.
    New York is one of the most **opulent** cities in the world.
    The farmer has an **opulent** crop of corn this year.

The noun, **opulence**:
    Read aloud: His **opulence** made him a powerful factor in the state.
    That writer is noted for his **opulence** of good phrases.

fraudulent   Guilty of trickery; dishonest; obtained by artifice or unfair methods.
    Read aloud: He obtained the old man's money by **fraudulent** means.
    His **fraudulent** purpose was thwarted by the police.
    It was a **fraudulent** story.

truculent   Fierce; savage; ferocious; cruel; violent; atrocious.
    (In the preferred pronunciation, the first syllable, **truc**, rhymes with **struck**. It is also correct to pronounce it **true**.)
    Read aloud: The maniac raved in a **truculent** manner.
    His voice was **truculent** as he denied the accusation.

somnolent   Sleepy; drowsy; inclined to sleep; inducing drowsiness.
    (It is pronounced: **som' no lent**.)
    Read aloud: I found myself in a **somnolent** mood.
    It was a **somnolent** talk that the professor gave.
    He always seems to have a **somnolent** expression on his face.

Practice
Use in sentences: **defraud**; **opulence**.

77

Words for Your Vocabulary

deride To make fun of; to laugh at with contempt; to turn to ridicule.

Read aloud: We **derided** him for wearing such conspicuous clothes.

He was **derided** for deserting his political party.

conjecture (*n.*) A guess; an inference or conclusion so drawn; state of being absorbed in making such an inference.

Read aloud: Remember that what I say about this case is only a **conjecture**.

For some moments he was lost in **conjecture**.

He refused to hazard a **conjecture**.

The verb:

Read aloud: We **conjectured** that he would visit us today.

The adjective, **conjectural**:

Read aloud: He was a **conjectural** critic.

All his opinions were **conjectural**.

insipid Without taste or flavor; wanting in spirit or animation; flat; dull; heavy.

(The accent must be placed on the second and not on the first syllable: in sip′ id.)

Read aloud: He had an **insipid** look even in the face of danger.

Instead of intelligent conversation, we were forced to listen to **insipid** chattering.

Practice

1. Give the noun form and the adjective form of **deride**.

2. Write two synonyms for: **insipid**; **impetuous**.

Pronunciation

gardenia   (gar dee′ nia *or* gar dee′ nyuh)
Note the sound of the second syllable. Do not say gar din′ i a.

eczema   (ek′ ze ma *or* ek′ se ma)
The accent should be on the first syllable. You have a choice of giving the second syllable a z or an s sound. Not ek zee′ ma.

long-lived   (lie′ vd)
This word should rhyme with **dived**. The i sounded like the **i** in **give** is also permitted.

zoology   (zoh ol′ o gy)
Focus attention on the sound of the first syllable. The **o** is pronounced like the **o** in **obey**. Do not say **zoo ol′ ogy**.

robot   (row′ bot *or* rob′ ot)
The trouble with the pronunciation of this word centers on the sound of the last syllable. Many, who think it is derived from the French language, refrain from sounding the final **t**. Do not have the second syllable rhyme with **flow**; rather, sound it like the first syllable in **bottle**.

quintuplets   **kwin′ tuplets, kwin tu′ plets or kwin tup′ lets**
We have Canada to thank for the popularity of this word. Formerly it had only one correct pronunciation. Now it would be difficult to mispronounce it.

tetanus   (tet′ anus)
This medical term for lockjaw must be accented on the first syllable, **tet**. It is never **tetan′ us**.

communiqué   (komu″ nikay′; *British,* komu′ nikay)
The last syllable receives the primary or principal accent; the second syllable, the secondary accent. One often hears it mispronounced **komunee′ kay**.

associate   (a so′ shi ate)
American dictionaries give only one form for the third syllable, **ci**, namely: **shi**. The third syllable of the noun form, **association,** may have the **si** sound or the **sh** sound.

Practice

Pronounce: **zoological; association; quadruplets; appreciation.**

79

Adjectives Ending in *tory*

predatory Pertaining to or characterized by plundering; robbing; addicted to pillaging.
(The primary accent is on the first syllable, **pred.**)

Read aloud: Drake and his men set out on a **predatory** excursion.

The men were sent to jail for their **predatory** acts.

contributory Tending, in common with other factors, to produce a result.
(Place the primary accent on the second syllable: **contrib' uto" ry.**)

Read aloud: His perseverance was a **contributory** cause of his success.

His disregard of the opinions of others was **contributory** to his failure.

defamatory Injurious to reputation; slanderous.
(Care must be taken in the pronunciation of this word. The primary accent is on the second syllable and not on the first: it is pronounced **defam' ato" ry** and not **def' amato" ry.** The accented syllable rhymes with **Sam.**)

Read aloud: The speaker regretted having used such **defamatory** words.

Defamatory reports were circulated about some of the political candidates.

mandatory Pertaining to an order or command; obligatory.
(In recent international law it has come to mean *having control and supervision over a small nation for the protection of the latter.*)

Read aloud: It was **mandatory** that schools be closed during the epidemic.

Such a **mandatory** measure was decried by the people.

Practice

Construct sentences with: **defame; mandate.**

LIBRARY
LUTHERAN BIBLE INSTITUTE
IN CALIFORNIA
641 S. WESTERN AVENUE
ANAHEIM, CA 92804

101

Meaningful Expressions

unflagging zeal
unflagging ambition

> (**unflagging**: Continuing with vigor.)
>
> *Read aloud:* Our people worked with **unflagging zeal** to purge the country of crime.
>
> His success was attributable to his **unflagging ambition**.

shallow observer
shallow remarks

> *Read aloud:* His article proved that he was only a **shallow observer** of human trends.
>
> No damage was done by his **shallow remarks**.

intemperate speech
intemperate use

> (**intemperate**: Not moderate or mild; ungovernable; inordinate.)
>
> *Read aloud:* His **intemperate speech** about our poor financial system was unjustified.
>
> There was no excuse for such **intemperate use** of profanity.

dogmatic utterance
dogmatic assurance

> (**dogmatic**: Asserting opinions as if one were the highest authority; positive; overbearing.)
>
> *Read aloud:* The people were growing tired of his **dogmatic utterances**.
>
> He attacked the plan with **dogmatic assurance**.

Practice

1. Use in sentences: **temper** (*v.*); **temperate**.

2. Write three synonyms for: **shallow**; **dogmatic**.

81

Words for Your Vocabulary

diversify   To give variety to; to make diverse or various in form or quality; to variegate.

(The i in the first syllable, **di,** may be pronounced like the i in **line** or like the i in **hit.**)

Read aloud: A good instructor can **diversify** his mode of teaching.

One should **diversify** his spare-time activities so that they will not be a continuation of his work day.

He is a man of **diversified** interests.

opprobrium   The disgrace that follows from, or is attached to, conduct that is considered evil or wrong; scorn; abuse; reproach mingled with contempt.

(The second syllable is **pro,** and should rhyme with **throw.**)

Read aloud: He deserved the **opprobrium** that fell upon him for accepting a bribe.

Benedict Arnold's name will always be spoken of with **opprobrium** in this country.

opinionated   Obstinate or conceited with regard to one's opinions; dogmatic.

Read aloud: He was too **opinionated** to be popular.

He was **opinionated** enough to tell his employer how to run the factory.

diction   Choice of words to express ideas; style of speaking or writing; the use of language with regard to accuracy or clearness.

Read aloud: A prize for the best **diction** is awarded each year to some radio announcer.

The primal object of this book is to improve your **diction.**

To be able to use good **diction** presupposes a knowledge of correct grammar and a reasonably large vocabulary.

Practice

Use in sentences: **divers** (*adj.*) ; **diverse**; **opprobrious.**

Self-Check No. Nine

Matching Exercise

Find in Column II a definition for each word in Column I.

I		II	
		a.	bold
		b.	charitable
1.	benevolent	*c.*	conclusive
2.	defamatory	*d.*	deceptive in appearance
3.	dexterous	*e.*	dishonest
4.	dogmatic	*f.*	greedy in eating
5.	fraudulent	*g.*	not moderate
6.	illusive	*h.*	obligatory
7.	impetuous	*i.*	positive
8.	insipid	*j.*	seditious
9.	intemperate	*k.*	severe
10.	mandatory	*l.*	skillful
11.	opprobrious	*m.*	slanderous
12.	opulent	*n.*	sleepy
13.	shallow	*o.*	superficial
14.	somnolent	*p.*	vehement in feeling
15.	voracious	*q.*	vile
		r.	wanting in spirit
		s.	wealthy

General Exercise

1. Construct sentences with: **truculent; diversify; derisive.**

2. What noun is related to **predatory?** (dep————)

3. Pronounce: **long-lived; zoology; robot.**

4. Have each of the following adjectives modify two nouns: **unflagging; dogmatic; callous.**

5. Use in sentences: **contributory; illusory; mandatory.**

6. Define: **diction; opinionated; delude.**

7. Pronounce: **associate** (*n.*); **quintuplets; eczema.**

8. Use in sentences: **benevolent; elusive.**

9. May a candidate receive a **plurality** of votes without having a **majority?**

10. Give two synonyms for: **dull; ridicule.**

82

Words Often Confused

emerge   To rise from; to come out into view; to become visible.

immerge   To plunge into, under, or within anything.

The prefixes in these two words are **e**, which means *from*, and **im**, which means *in* or *into*. If this fact is remembered, no confusion of these two words will ever be experienced.

   Read aloud: He is gradually **immerging** into trouble.

      Such riotous spending is bound to **immerge** us in debt.

      We are gradually **emerging** from the depression.

      Our party **emerged** from the conflict better and stronger than ever.

      The Yankees showed signs of **emerging** from a batting slump.

respectable   Worthy of respect or esteem; fair in size or quantity.

respectful   Full of respect; showing deference.

respective   Relating to particular persons or things, each to each.

These are three inoffensive-looking words, but nevertheless there may be a little dynamite stored in them to cause trouble when we endeavor to use them.

   Read aloud: We won by a **respectable** margin.

      This city is noted for its **respectable** citizens.

      I received a **respectful** bow from my adversary.

      The people then departed for their **respective** homes.

Practice

1. Construct sentences with: **merge; emergence.**

2. Illustrate the meaning of: **immerse; immersion.**

83

Words for Your Vocabulary

submissive   Inclined or ready to submit; yielding; obedient; humble.
Read aloud: There was a **submissive** tone in his request.
As a child he was very **submissive**.

graphic   Clearly and vividly written or told; characterized by clear and impressing description; of or about diagrams and their use.
Read aloud: He gave a **graphic** description of the play.
He has always been considered a **graphic** writer.
The paper contains a **graphic** account of the meeting.

bellicose   Warlike; inclined to contention; fond of fighting; pugnacious.
(The accent may be on the first syllable or on the last syllable: **bel' i kose** or **bel i kose'**.)
Read aloud: He was in a **bellicose** mood when we met him.
A more **bellicose** people would be difficult to find.

culpable   Deserving censure or moral blame; faulty; immoral; blameworthy.
(It is pronounced **kul' pa ble**.)
Read aloud: Evidence pointed to Skinner as the **culpable** one.
He was found **culpable** of the charge.
The driver of the bus was in no way **culpable** for the accident.

Practice

1. Use in sentences: **submit; culpability**.

2. Give two synonyms for **bellicose** and use them in sentences.

3. What is the meaning of **belligerent?**

84

Adjectives

ponderous   Of great weight; oppressively heavy; dull; labored.

(Two pronunciations for this word are found in *Webster's New International Dictionary* (2nd ed.): **pon′ der us** and **pon′ drus.** It may have three or two syllables.)

Read aloud: He carried a **ponderous** weight on his back.

His style is too **ponderous** to be entertaining.

The jokes were **ponderous** and dry.

sedulous   Diligent; hard working; persevering; industrious.

(It is pronounced as if spelled **sed′ ju lus.**)

Read aloud: He is a **sedulous** student.

By **sedulous** application he managed to become head of the firm.

seditious   Stirring up discontent or rebellion; tending to excite; disposed to arouse; turbulent; factious.

Read aloud: The people were astounded at his **seditious** speech.

The **seditious** citizens were finally arrested.

Seditious literature was disseminated by the agitators.

risible   Causing laughter; funny; disposed to laugh; pertaining to laughter.

(Pronounce the first syllable **riz,** thus: **riz′ a ble.**)

Read aloud: He has such an angry-looking face, I am sure it does not have any **risible** muscles.

They soon learned that I was not in a **risible** mood.

Practice

1. Use in sentences: **derision; imponderable.**

2. Give two antonyms for **sedulous.**

3. What is the noun form of **seditious?**

85

Adjectives Ending in *ative*

Read aloud the following sentences and then construct sentences of your own with the given words. It is correct to pronounce these words with or without a secondary accent; thus, **appreciative** may be **appre' shiative** or **appre' shi a" tiv.**

appreciative   Showing esteem, interest, sympathy.
    Read aloud: I found him a very **appreciative** person.
    We played to an **appreciative** audience.

legislative   Pertaining to, or enacted by, law.
    Read aloud: The **legislative** assembly will meet next week.
    Only **legislative** business was discussed.

illustrative   Serving as an example.
    Read aloud: The teacher had much **illustrative** material on the table.
    This paper is **illustrative** of what he can do in Latin.

imitative   Given to copying others; formed after a model.
    Read aloud: He is an **imitative** boy.
    Acting is an **imitative** art.

administrative   Pertaining to the management of affairs or government.
    Read aloud: His **administrative** work is becoming very burdensome.
    You will find Mr. Jones in the **administrative** office.

remunerative   Pertaining to compensation or reward.
    Read aloud: You will soon realize that vocabulary building is a **remunerative** subject.
    He is now engaged in a **remunerative** undertaking.

demonstrative   Showing one's feelings; exhibiting conclusively.
    Read aloud: Don't you think he is too **demonstrative?**
    It was a **demonstrative** meeting.

Practice

1. Use in sentences: **appreciable; remunerate.**

2. What is the verb form of: **legislative; imitative?**

3. Construct sentences with: **administer; legislate.**

108

86

Words for Your Vocabulary

coerce
　　　　To compel; to force; to constrain by force, especially by law or authority.
　　　　(Pronounced: **ko urs'**. The last syllable rhymes with **hearse**.)
Read aloud: They were **coerced** into contributing to the campaign fund.
They tried to **coerce** him into stealing.

The adjective, **coercive**:
Read aloud: **Coercive** measures were used to make the Colonists pay heavy taxes.
Coercive obedience is far inferior to voluntary obedience.

The noun, **coercion**:
Read aloud: No amount of **coercion** could make the martyr renounce his religion.
That end will be attained only by **coercion**.

symbolize
　　　　To represent or express by a symbol; to stand for; to typify.
Read aloud: The constant roar of the factory machines **symbolized** the return of good times.
That diploma **symbolizes** many years of study.

The adjective, **symbolic**:
Read aloud: A diamond ring on that finger is **symbolic** of an engagement.
The lamb is **symbolic** of gentleness.

calumniate
　　　　To slander; to accuse falsely of a crime or offense; to say injurious things about; to libel.
　　　　(It is pronounced **ka lum' ni ate**. The first **a** is like that in **account**; the last syllable rhymes with **fate**.)
Read aloud: The two speakers **calumniated** each other during the campaign.
To **calumniate** anyone is a mark of inferiority in the speaker.

Practice
What is the adjectival form of **calumniate**?

Related Words *(lud* or *lus)*

Our language is full of words which carry the idea of *deception* or *deceit*. While they are apparently the same in meaning, close study will reveal differences.

delude

To lead from the truth or into error; to mislead; to trick.

Read aloud: It is often easy to **delude** old people.

The country was **deluded** by his visionary schemes.

delusion

That which is falsely believed; a misleading of the mind.

Read aloud: If you think it is difficult to increase your vocabulary, you are laboring under a **delusion**.

The new religious sect clung to the **delusion** that the end of the world was near.

delusive

False; deceptive; beguiling.

Read aloud: That politician harbors many **delusive** ideas.

For him to think that he could continue to violate the traffic laws was **delusive** reasoning.

elude

To avoid slyly or adroitly; to evade; to escape the notice of.

(Note that this word and its derivatives have the meaning of cleverness or agility.)

Read aloud: The boy **eluded** the blow that was directed at him.

We were unable to **elude** the vigilant eye of the detective

Practice

1. Have **elusive** modify three nouns.

2. Is there a difference between **illusion** and **delusion?** Prove your answer.

88

Adjectives Ending in *ious*

usurious Taking extremely high or unlawful rate of inter-
est.
(Some dictionaries give two pronunciations for
this word. *Webster's New International Dic-
tionary* (2nd ed.) has only one: **u zhoor' i us.**
Some dictionaries also give: **u zu' ri us.**)
Read aloud: Such **usurious** practice should be abolished by
the courts.
He was called a **usurious** lender.
The contract was **usurious.**

envious Wishing to have something someone else has;
actuated by envy; maliciously grudging.
Read aloud: Many were **envious** of the honors accorded the
executive.
The fact that the critics are **envious** accounts for their hostile editorials.
The happy man is he who is not **envious** of his neighbor's
wealth or any other worldly possessions.

Another adjective, **enviable:**
Read aloud: John established an **enviable** record at college as
a football player.
He has an **enviable** vocabulary.

melodious Sweet-sounding; agreeable to the ear by a sweet
succession of sounds; musical.
Read aloud: **Melodious** strains were carried by the breeze.
She has a **melodious** voice.
The word that he was to be president of the concern was
melodious news to him.

penurious Excessively sparing in the use of money; stingy;
miserly.
(Be careful of the sound of the second syllable,
nu. It is pronounced like the **u** in **cube,** and
not like the **oo** in **food: pe nu' ri us.** Care
must be taken in regard to its meaning.
Though the noun **penury** means *very great
want,* **penurious** denotes *stinginess.*)
Read aloud: He was too **penurious** to dress well.
His **penurious** ways alienated his friends.

Practice
What are the noun forms for the words in this lesson?

Meaningful Expressions

trenchant editorial
trenchant tongue

    (**trenchant**: Cutting; sharp; keen.)

Read aloud: It was a **trenchant editorial** against his policy.
We did our best to escape his **trenchant tongue.**

pungent remarks
pungent odor

    (**pungent**: Causing a sharp sensation; piercing; stabbing; stinging; caustic.)

Read aloud: His sermon was punctuated with **pungent remarks** about the laxity of our police.
The **pungent odor** of fall flowers was in the room.

responsive note
responsive audience

    (**responsive**: Ready or inclined to respond; easily moved; responding readily.)

Read aloud: His speech struck a **responsive note** in his listeners.
The actor found the **audience** very **responsive.**

intrenched hatred
intrenched hope

Read aloud: The ruler accomplished very little, owing to the **intrenched hatred** of his subjects.
A **hope** firmly **intrenched** in my heart is that you will be able to follow in your father's steps.

lethargic person
lethargic temperament

    (**lethargic**: Morbidly drowsy; sluggish; dull; heavy. Accent the second syllable: **lethar′gic.**)

Read aloud: We never met a more **lethargic person** than he.
Speed or haste was foreign to his **lethargic temperament.**

90

Words for Your Vocabulary

defection   A falling away from loyalty, duty, etc.; deser‑
tion; apostasy.
Read aloud: There was **defection** in the army when the lead‑
ers were changed.
According to newspaper reports, there was **defection** in the
political ranks before election day.

refractory   Obstinate; not yielding; disobedient; unman‑
ageable; difficult to melt or draw out, as metal,
etc.
(In pronouncing this word, you should place the
stress on the second **r**; otherwise, you may be
inclined to pronounce it **refactory**.)
Read aloud: The **refractory** child deserved to be punished.
I have had a **refractory** cold all winter.
The workers were discussing the various **refractory** ores and
metals.

deduce   To draw a conclusion from a general rule or prin‑
ciple; to derive by logical process.
(Accent the last syllable: **deduce'**.)
Read aloud: From what he said, I **deduced** that he wished to
become president of the bank.
Because of his many law infractions and arrests, we **deduced**
that he would not be an asset to any city.

The noun, **deduction**:
Read aloud: The **deduction** was that he would take the posi‑
tion if it was offered.
From his statements, the **deduction** was made that he be‑
lieved Johnson guilty.

Practice

1. Use in sentences: **fractious; deducible; fragment;
deduction.**

2. Write three words whose last syllable is **duce.**

3. Give synonyms for: **sluggish; preliminary; reward**
(*v.*); **pugnacious; false; sympathetic; conclusive; typify;
management.**

Self-Check No. Ten

Selection Exercise

Each word at the left is correctly defined by one of the three words opposite it. Find and check the correct definition for each word at the left:

1. **risible** . . . . ___foolish ___laughable ___light
2. **sedulous** . . . . . . ___persevering ___sitting ___slow
3. **ponderous** . . . . . ___forceful ___labored ___meditative
4. **seditious** . . . . . . ___convenient ___factious ___sickly
5. **coerce** . . . . ___accuse ___compel ___link
6. **graphic** . . . . ___clear ___musical ___statistical
7. **culpable** . . . . . . ___blameless ___faulty ___free
8. **submissive** . . . . . ___despatch ___underhanded ___yielding
9. **deduce** . . . . ___derive ___lose ___mislead
10. **refractory** . . . . . ___excitable ___injury ___obstinate
11. **defection** . . . . . . ___desertion ___meal ___sickness
12. **penurious** . . . . . ___dishonest ___miserly ___poor
13. **calumniate** . . . . . ___force ___libel ___mistreat
14. **pungent** . . . . ___caustic ___stingy ___sweet
15. **remunerative** . . ___expensive ___illegal ___paying

General Exercise

1. Illustrate the meaning of: **emerge; immerge.**

2. Write three words related to **delude.**

3. What is the noun form of **seditious?**

4. How does **respectful** differ in meaning from **respectable?**

5. Have each adjective modify two nouns: **graphic; demonstrative; lethargic.**

6. Construct sentences with: **envious; culpable; deduce; elusive.**

7. Give a synonym for each of the following:

sluggish	cutting	reward (*v.*)
pugnacious	false	management
sympathetic	typify	

114

91

Words Often Confused

assimilate To absorb or appropriate, as nourishment; tc make similar.

simulate To assume or have the mere appearance of; to pretend; to feign; to imitate.
(Note that the second syllable is **u** and not **i**: sim' u late.)

Read aloud: He finds it difficult to **assimilate** what he reads.
We **assimilated** our program to the program of last year.
The class **simulated** an interest in chemistry.
The loyalty they manifested was only **simulated**.

complacent Satisfied; especially, self-satisfied; pleased with oneself.
(It is pronounced: **kom play' sent**.)

complaisant Disposed to please; courteous; obliging; com pliant.
(It may have the accent on the second or on the first syllable: **kom play' zant** or **kom' play zant**. It is also correct to say **kom play' sant**.)

Read aloud: They seem to be a **complacent** people.
A **complacent** smile was registered on his countenance.
He listened to the story in a **complaisant** manner.
One may be **complacent** without being **complaisant**.

penurious Excessively sparing in the use of money; stingy.
(Note the sound of the second syllable: **pe new' ri us**.)

impecunious Not having money; poor.
(It is pronounced: **im pe kew' ni us**.)

Read aloud: He was so **penurious** that he would scarcely buy sufficient food for his family.
The man's **impecunious** state aroused our sympathy and charity.

Practice

1. Construct sentences with: **assimilation; simulation**.
2. What is the meaning of: **penury; complacency?**

92

Nouns Ending in *tion*

There are many words in our language whose noun forms
end in **tion,** which means *act of, state of being,* or *result of.*
Here are a few that will enhance your vocabulary.

disruption   A breaking up; a split; state of being rent
          asunder; a breach.
    Read aloud: What caused the **disruption** of his family?
    There will be a **disruption** in that political party before
    many months.

  The verb, **disrupt:**
    Read aloud: His loud laughter almost **disrupted** the meeting.
    The presence of the police **disrupted** the fiery meeting of
    the strikers.

corruption   A decay; evil conduct; impairment of integrity,
          virtue, or moral principle; dishonesty; act of
          changing for the worse.
    Read aloud: The minister decried the **corruption** that existed
    in politics.
    He spoke about the **corruption** of the body after death.
    That there is today a **corruption** of our language by the
    youth of the country cannot be denied.

  The verb, **corrupt:**
    Read aloud: They quickly learned that they could not **corrupt**
    the jury.

  The adjective, **corrupt:**
    Read aloud: The lawyer was disbarred because of **corrupt**
    practice.
    The **corrupt** agent was sent to jail.

pollution   Uncleanness; defilement; impurity.
    Read aloud: The disease was traced to **pollution** of the source
    of the drinking water.
    Pollution of politics is likely to increase with the indiffer-
    ence of the public.

Practice

Use in sentences: **disrupt; corrupt; pollute.**

93

Adjectives

inflammatory   Tending to excite anger, tumult, animosity. Medically, it means accompanied by, or tending to cause, inflammation.

(It is pronounced: inflam′ mato″ ry. The second syllable flam must rhyme with slam and not with blame.)

Read aloud: Such **inflammatory** speeches should never be permitted.

His **inflammatory** writings caused great unrest.

He has an **inflammatory** disease.

dilatory   Tending to delay; characterized by slowness; tardy.

Read aloud: The **dilatory** policy of that country proved very costly.

Her payments on the house were **dilatory**.

invidious   Tending to excite ill will or envy; liable to give offense.

(It is pronounced: in vid′ i us.)

Read aloud: Such comparisons are **invidious**.

The distinctions were too **invidious** to be accepted.

We took exception to his **invidious** remarks.

fastidious   Hard to please; dainty in taste; overnice; delicate to a fault.

(It has four syllables: fas tid′ i us.)

Read aloud: She has a **fastidious** appetite.

He is too **fastidious** in his use of grammar.

He has a **fastidious** taste.

Practice

Construct sentences with: **dilate; inflame.**

94

Adjectives Ending in *ious*

The adjective suffix **ious** means *full of* or *characterized by*. The **ious** words in this lesson are formed from nouns ending in **ion**.

factious   Fond of party strife; stirring up disputes; addicted to forming parties to raise dissensions; seditious.

                (Pronounced: **fak′ shus.**)

Read aloud: The meeting was spoiled by **factious** quarrels.

There is a **factious** element in our group.

pretentious   Making or possessing claims to excellence, greatness, merit, etc.; showy; ostentatious; pompous.

                (The **ti** has an **sh** sound: **pre ten′ shus.**)

Read aloud: They now live in a very **pretentious** home.

We were entertained in a **pretentious** way.

The speakers were too **pretentious,** and as a result failed to win many followers.

infectious   Having qualities that may spread; communicable; catching; capable of being diffused; sympathetic.

                (Pronounce it: **in fek′ shus.**)

Read aloud: There are many **infectious** diseases in the tropical countries.

The teacher's enthusiasm was **infectious.**

Their mirth was **infectious.**

contentious   Quarrelsome; given to altercation or controversy; characterized by heated argument or statement.

                (It is pronounced: **kon ten′ shus.**)

Read aloud: His friends were very **contentious** at the ball game and seemed to question every decision of the umpire.

This will be a **contentious** issue if brought before the people.

His **contentious** spirit made him an unwelcome guest wherever he appeared.

118

95

Words for Your Vocabulary

repudiate   To cast off; to disown; to refuse to accept; to refuse to pay.

Read aloud: The father did not **repudiate** the prodigal son.

They **repudiated** my offer for the property.

Jones has **repudiated** his debts.

The noun, **repudiation**:

Read aloud: The depression years were an era of **repudiation**.

You have read about the **repudiation** of the war debts by some of the European countries.

efficacy   Power to produce effects or desired results.

(The accent must be placed on the first syllable: **ef' i ka si**.)

Read aloud: He believes in the **efficacy** of prayer.

That religious body does not believe in the **efficacy** of medicine.

He spoke in reference to the **efficacy** of a strong vocabulary.

The adjective, **efficacious**, is pronounced: **ef i kay' shus**:

Read aloud: The remedy proved **efficacious**.

It was an **efficacious** law.

tenacious   Holding fast; inclined to retain what is in possession; able to retain.

Read aloud: The people were **tenacious** of their rights.

The professor has a **tenacious** memory.

The dog had a **tenacious** grip on my trousers.

The noun, **tenacity**:

Read aloud: He should be commended for his **tenacity** of purpose.

Backward countries cling to old customs with **tenacity**.

Practice

Give two synonyms for **repudiate**.

96

Pronunciation

gratis   (gray′ tis or grat′ is)
The Latin form **grah′ tis** has not yet been sanctioned by the dictionary makers. The first syllable should rhyme with **day** or with **cat.**

root   (root)
This word has two forms. It may rhyme with **boot** or with **foot.**

column   (kol′ um)
There is no **y** sound in this word. To pronounce it **kol′ yum** is absolutely incorrect.

decade   (dek′ aid)
The accent is on the first syllable, and the second syllable rhymes with **paid. Decayed′** is the British form.

corps   (kor)
This word rhymes with **fore.** Do not pronounce it as though it were spelled **corpse.**

alias   (ay′ lee us)
Note that the accent is on the first syllable. Do not say **a lie′ us.**

expert (*adj.*)   (ex′ pert or expert′)
This adjective may be accented on the first or the last syllable.

apparatus   (apparay′ tus or apparat′ us)
It is correct to have the third syllable rhyme with **bay** or with **cat.**

enervate   (en′ ervate or ener′ vate)
The accent may be placed on the first or the second syllable.

Practice

Construct sentences with: **decade; gratis; alias; enervate.**

Words with the Prefix *trans*

translate   To change from one language into another; to change from one position or condition to another.

(Accent the last syllable: **translate'**.)

Read aloud: He could not **translate** a passage from Cicero.

I wish you could **translate** your thoughts into acts.

transcend   To go beyond; to be higher or greater than; to be far superior to.

(Accent the last syllable: **transcend'**.)

Read aloud: The beauty of the landscape **transcends** description.

The results have **transcended** my highest expectations.

transcendent   Superior; surpassing; extraordinary.

Read aloud: She was a woman of **transcendent** beauty.

The mayor is of **transcendent** worth to this city.

His **transcendent** selfishness resulted in his ruin.

transact   To carry on business; to have dealings; to carry through; to bring about.

(The last syllable should be accented.)

Read aloud: He did not wish to **transact** affairs with his enemy.

He **transacted** his business efficiently and profitably.

transpire   To leak out; to come to light; to perspire.

(The accent is on the last syllable: **transpire'**. Do not use this word in the sense "to happen; to occur," as most authorities on usage disapprove of it. It may be a surprise to many that this word also means "to perspire.")

Read aloud: What happened at their meeting soon **transpired**.

It **transpired** that one of our army officials was a spy.

Practice

Use in sentences: **ascendant; ascendancy; transmit; transaction.**

98

Meaningful Expressions

supercilious look
supercilious manner
> (**supercilious**: Haughty; proud; disdainful; contemptuous.)
> *Read aloud:* My employer gave me a **supercilious look** when I spoke out of turn.
> Her **supercilious manner** alienated her friends.

staggering debt
staggering demands
> *Read aloud:* His **staggering debt** eventually affected his mind.
> He was unable to meet the **staggering demands** of his family.

mangled report
mangled remains
> (**mangled**: Mutilated; torn; lacerated; spoiled.)
> *Read aloud:* It was a **mangled report** we received from our correspondent in the war zone.
> The **mangled remains** of the victim were not recognizable.

inconceivable cruelty
inconceivable blunder
> (**inconceivable**: Impossible to imagine; unthinkable; hard to believe; incredible.)
> *Read aloud:* He was roughly handled for his **inconceivable cruelty** to his help.
> For his **inconceivable blunder** of arresting the mayor, the chief was forced to resign.

perennial complaint
perennial joke
> (**perennial**: Lasting or recurring from year to year or through a series of years.)
> *Read aloud:* His **perennial complaint** about the poor condition of the streets was received yesterday.
> That is one of his **perennial jokes.**

Words for Your Vocabulary

senile

Pertaining to, or characteristic of, old age; exhibiting, or proceeding from, old age.

(There are two pronunciations for **senile**: **see′ nile** and **see′ nil**. The last syllable in the first form rhymes with **mile**; in the second form, it rhymes with **pill**.)

Read aloud: His suffering is due principally to **senile** infirmity.

He is too **senile** to attempt that kind of work.

Senile pleasures are simple and few.

sinecure

Any office or position of value which requires or involves little or no responsibility; easy and well-paying job with little work attached.

(There are two pronunciations for this word: **sye′ ne kure** and **sin′ e kure**. The first syllable in the first form rhymes with **pie**; the first in the second form rhymes with **pin**.)

Read aloud: Most of the **sinecures** were distributed among the politicians who worked diligently during the campaign.

Serving as secretary to the mayor is by no means a **sinecure**.

ingratiate

To bring (oneself) into favor; to introduce or commend to favor.

(It is pronounced as though it were spelled **in gray′ shi ate**.)

Read aloud: His faithfulness **ingratiated** him with his superiors.

John tried to **ingratiate** himself with Bob by inviting him to the theater.

The noun, **ingratitude,** has no connection with **ingratiate**. The former means *ill return for kindness; lack of thankfulness:*

Read aloud: Through his **ingratitude** he lost many close friends.

epitome

A condensed account; a brief or curtailed statement of the contents of a topic or a work; a summary.

(There are four syllables in this word. It is pronounced: **e pit′ o mee**. Never say **ep′ i tome**.)

Read aloud: He gave an **epitome** of the book.

This is an **epitome** of life on a farm.

Self-Check No. Eleven

Completion Exercise

Nouns		Verbs	Adjectives	
complacency	efficacy	conciliate	complacent	pretentious
contention	epitome	ingratiate	dilatory	senile
corruption	sinecure	repudiate	efficacious	staggering
disruption	tenacity	simulate	fastidious	supercilious
			inflammatory	tenacious
			mangled	

Fill each blank below with an appropriate word from the above list. Do not use the same word twice.

1. He believes in the _____ of prayer.
2. She is very _____ about her dress.
3. He had a(n) _____ grip on the robber's throat.
4. He was asked to give a(n) _____ of the book.
5. Much _____ has been found in this world.
6. The office of mayor is by no means a(n) _____.
7. His _____ remarks caused an outburst of laughter.
8. His _____ speech was justly condemned.
9. He tried to _____ himself with his superior.
10. He is very _____ in paying his debts.
11. They _____ my offer for the property.
12. There will soon be _____ in their political ranks.
13. He was disliked for his _____ manner.
14. The new tax is a point of much _____.
15. His _____ claims to nobility are without foundation.

General Exercise

1. Give two pronunciations for **decade.**

2. Pronounce: **alias; column; root.**

3. Construct sentences with: **factious; infectious.**

4. How does **complacent** differ in meaning from **complaisant?**

5. Define and explain the origin of: **perennial; supercilious.**

100

Words Often Confused

debar	To shut out; to prevent; to hinder from enjoyment; to prohibit.
	(The last syllable is accented: **de bar′.**)
disbar	To expel from the legal profession.

Read aloud: The fact that he was born in Europe **debarred** him from the presidency of the United States.

His low wages **debarred** him from enjoying many of the pleasures of life.

The lawyer was **disbarred** for corrupt legal practice.

urban	Pertaining to a city or town; characteristic of cities.
	(The **a** has the sound of **a** in **account.** The accent is on the first syllable: **er′ ban.**)
urbane	Courteous; polite; refined.
	(The second syllable **bane** rhymes with **cane.** Note that the accent is on the last syllable, **er bane′.**)

Read aloud: The **urban** population is many times greater than the rural population.

The country boy soon learned our **urban** customs.

He found the people **urbane** and hospitable.

I should like to cultivate Mr. Reynold's **urbane** manner.

turgid	Swollen; bloated; inflated; pompous.
turbid	Muddy; having the sediment disturbed; not clean; polluted.

Read aloud: The **turgid** streams caused considerable damage.

His style was **turgid** and uninteresting.

The brook was so **turbid** that we could not see bottom.

His **turbid** stories were not favorably received by the audience.

Practice

1. Construct sentences with: **urbanity; disbarment.**

2. Note the different sound of **a** in **urban** and **urbane.**

101

Related Words *(potent)*

Ability to use words derived from the Latin word **possum,** *I can* or *I am able,* will greatly improve one's diction.

potential   Existing in possibility, not in actuality; capable of coming into being or action.

(It means that the person has shown signs or earmarks of attaining the objective mentioned, whether it be good or bad.)

Read aloud: He is a **potential** football player.

Jones is one of the **potential** candidates for the senatorship.

His disregard for law and order when he was young indicated that he was a **potential** criminal.

potent   Having great power; mighty; influential.

Read aloud: He was a **potent** factor for good in the community.

The drink was too **potent** for me.

He presented a **potent** argument against atheism.

impotent   Not having power; helpless.

(Care should be taken in the pronunciation of this word. The accent must be on the first syllable: **im′ potent.** Never say **impo′ tent.**)

Read aloud: Man without God is absolutely **impotent.**

The **impotent** ruler was the cause of the revolution.

Practice

1.   Write three more words that belong to the **potent** family of words.

2.   Construct sentences with the noun form of: **impotent; potential.**

102

Adjectives

mundane Of or pertaining to the world; worldly; not con-
cerned with church or spiritual things.
(It is pronounced: **mun' dane**, the last syllable
rhyming with **plane**.)
Read aloud: **Mundane** pleasures are at best short-lived.
He is concerned only with **mundane** affairs.
Use in sentences: **mundane happiness; mundane suffering;
mundane reward; mundane eyes.**

recondite Hidden from sight; concealed; beyond the view
of average intelligence; characterized by pro-
found scholarship.
(This word has two pronunciations: **rek' un dite**
and **re kon' dite**. The last syllable in each
case should rhyme with **kite**.)
Read aloud: His books are all of a **recondite** nature.
The talk was too **recondite** for the audience.
Use in sentences: **recondite machinery; recondite writing;
recondite subject; recondite aspirations.**

abortive Coming to naught; failing in its effect; fruitless;
unsuccessful.
Read aloud: It proved to be an **abortive** undertaking.
All efforts to rescue him were **abortive**.
Use in sentences: **abortive attempt; abortive enterprise;
abortive project; abortive speech.**

punitive Concerned with penalties or punishment; inflict-
ing punishment.
(The **u** is long, as in **use: pu' ni tive**.)
Read aloud: The automobile laws should be more **punitive**.
It turned out to be a **punitive** expedition.
The transgressor eventually realizes that justice is **punitive**.

Practice

Use in sentences the antonyms for: **mundane; recondite.**

103

"C" Adjectives

As a diversion from the customary mode of word study, try to evolve as many adjectives as possible that begin with the same letter. The following adjectives belong to the "C"-family. Some of them you have already seen, but inasmuch as they are of a practical nature, a little repetition may be beneficial. The words will be briefly defined.

capacious   Roomy; able to hold much.
Read aloud: The child has a **capacious** memory for names.
We could not find a hall **capacious** enough to accommodate the delegates.

cumbrous   Burdensome; unwieldy.
Read aloud: The weight was too **cumbrous** for him to carry.
Try to avoid the use of long, **cumbrous** expressions.

capricious   Apt to change suddenly; irregular.
Read aloud: It was difficult to tolerate her **capricious** nature.
The weather for the past month has been **capricious**.

conclusive   Decisive; convincing; final.
Read aloud: There was **conclusive** evidence that Brown stole the jewelry.
The proof that he was guilty was **conclusive**.

contrite   Penitent; broken in spirit by a sense of guilt.
(Accent the first syllable: kon' trite.)
Read aloud: The letter was couched in **contrite** words.
It was with **contrite** heart that he confessed his part in the crime.

circuitous   Roundabout; not direct.
Read aloud: We took a **circuitous** route to New York.
His explanation was so **circuitous** that it was difficult to understand him.

Practice

1. Construct sentences with: **crucial; conspicuous; congenial; cynical; chivalrous; calamitous.**

2. How do you pronounce **circuit?**

3. Write the noun form of: **contrite; capricious; capacious.**

104

Words for Your Vocabulary

constrain   To compel; to force; to necessitate; to produce in an unnatural manner.
Read aloud: We were **constrained** to work in order to live.
I am **constrained** to tell you that your services are no longer required.

The noun, **constraint**:
Read aloud: Too many **constraints** have been placed upon that child.
He visited me by **constraint**.

debility   Weakness; feebleness; languor.
Read aloud: Age is the cause of his general **debility**.
He realized his **debility** in word study.

momentous   Very important; weighty; of moment or consequence.
Read aloud: The Supreme Court must soon make a **momentous** decision.
It was a **momentous** occasion for the young actor.
He took that private passage which he had trod so often in less **momentous** hours.

generate   To produce; to bring into life; to cause.
Read aloud: That engine cannot **generate** enough heat.
She **generates** happiness wherever she goes.
He is **generating** a false impression of our troubles.

intelligible   Capable of being understood or comprehended.
Read aloud: The child gave an **intelligible** account of himself
His answers were not **intelligible**.
The baby's talk is fast becoming **intelligible**.

Practice

1. Use in sentences: **momentary; momentous**.
2. Construct sentences with: **constraint; unintelligible**.

Pronunciation

incongruous (in kon' groo us)
Characterized by lack of harmony or consistency;
inconsistent; inharmonious; not appropriate.

Pronounce it **in kon' groo us.** The **oo** is as in **foot.**

Read aloud: She told an **incongruous** story to the court.
Those colors are **incongruous.**
Overcoats are **incongruous** on a warm day.
Use in sentences: **incongruous** style; **incongruous** statements; **incongruous** acts; **incongruous** desires.

respite (res' pit)
A putting off; postponement; temporary intermission of labor.

There are two things to remember about this word: the accent is on the first syllable, and the second syllable rhymes with **sit** and not with **kite.** Say **res' pit,** not **ree spite'.**

Read aloud: The soldiers received a **respite** from fighting.
No **respite** was given the brave firemen during the con flagration.

lamentable (lam' entable)
Mournful; sorrowful; expressing grief; deplorable; pitiable.

This is another of those words which are mispronounced more frequently than they are pronounced correctly. In this word, the accent must be placed on the first and not the second syllable: **lam' entable,** not **lament' able.**

Read aloud: He committed a **lamentable** mistake.
His countenance wore a **lamentable** expression.
Joseph was a **lamentable** failure at college.
The football team made a **lamentable** showing against Yale.
Use in sentences: **lamentable** weakness; **lamentable** attempt; **lamentable** tale; **lamentable** error.

106

Verbs Ending in *ize*

Have you ever paused to examine your stock of words that end in **ize?** Our language verily teems with them. Try to incorporate the following words in your speaking or active vocabulary. You will find them both euphonious and practical.

authorize　　To clothe with authority or legal power; to justify; to give authority for.

Read aloud: The president of the firm **authorized** me to buy two trucks.

He was **authorized** to spend a large sum of money for relief work.

signalize　　To make known; to mark or display conspicuously; to point out carefully or distinctly.

Read aloud: The re-opening of our factories **signalizes** the return of good times.

The advent of autumn was **signalized** by the multicolored foliage of the trees.

jeopardize　　To expose to loss or injury; to risk; to endanger; to imperil.

(The first syllable is pronounced **jep.**)

Read aloud: If he were seen in your company, his chance for promotion might be **jeopardized.**

He **jeopardizes** his life each time he enters an automobile race.

The noun, **jeopardy:**
Read aloud: The millionaire's life was always in **jeopardy.**

minimize　　To reduce to the smallest part or proportion possible; to make the least of.

Read aloud: He tried to **minimize** the extent of his crime.

Practice

Use in sentences: **signal** (*adj.*); **jeopardy; symbolize; authorization.**

107

Nouns Ending in *tion*

assumption   Assuming; act of taking upon oneself; appropriation; usurpation; unwarrantable pretentiousness; arrogance.

(It is now permissible, according to *Webster's New International Dictionary* (2nd ed.), to pronounce or not to pronounce the **p.** It may be **a sump' shun,** or **a sum' shun.**)

Read aloud: What occasioned the **assumption** of authority by him?

He has agreed to the **assumption** of all his brother's debts.

She appeared at the conference with an air of **assumption** that was almost ridiculous.

ebullition   State of boiling or bubbling up; agitation or excitement; sudden burst of violent display.

(The **u** has the sound of the **u** in **circus**: **eb u lish' un.**)

Read aloud: What caused this **ebullition** of anger on the part of Jones?

His appearance brought forth an **ebullition** of applause.

The talk seemed to be the **ebullition** of some immature mind.

recognition   State of being recognized; acknowledgment for services rendered; favorable notice.

(Focus your attention on the second syllable **og;** the **g** is not silent. The word is pronounced **rek" og nish' un,** and not **rek" on nish' un.**)

Read aloud: Neither of the two persons gave any sign of **recognition.**

In **recognition** of his faithful work, he received a substantial gift.

The author, by persevering at his work, finally won **recognition** from the public.

Practice

1. Use in sentences: **assumption; recognition.**
2. Construct sentences with: **recognizable.**

108

Words for Your Vocabulary

deter To turn aside; to discourage; to keep back; to hinder.
(Accent the last syllable: **deter'**.)
Read aloud: Nothing will **deter** me from my purpose.
Rain **deterred** us from going to New York yesterday.

The noun, **deterrent**:
Read aloud: Lack of funds was the **deterrent** to our going on a vacation.
The only **deterrent** to his coming will be ill-health.

rejuvenate To render young or youthful again; to reinvigorate; to impart new vitality to.
Read aloud: The European trip **rejuvenated** my brother.
The victory **rejuvenated** the enthusiasm of years ago.

invigorate To give strength to; to animate; to fill with life and vigor.
Read aloud: The ocean trip seemed to **invigorate** Mr. Brown.
The return of good times has **invigorated** the hopes of mankind.

The adjective, **invigorating**:
Read aloud: Golf is an **invigorating** game.
We listened to an **invigorating** talk on economics.

disintegrate To break up; to reduce or become reduced to small fragments; to destroy the unity or wholeness of.
Read aloud: The organization is beginning to **disintegrate**.
In some countries, the social structure has practically **disintegrated**.

Practice

Place in sentences: **deterrent**; **integrate**; **placate**; **juvenile**.

Self-Check No. Twelve

Adjective Exercise

Have each adjective qualify two nouns:

1. mundane   ------------------   ------------------
2. abortive   ------------------   ------------------
3. potent   ------------------   ------------------
4. momentous   ------------------   ------------------
5. capacious   ------------------   ------------------
6. potential   ------------------   ------------------
7. incongruous   ------------------   ------------------
8. lamentable   ------------------   ------------------
9. cumbrous   ------------------   ------------------
10. circuitous   ------------------   ------------------

Completion Exercise

Complete the spelling of the word in parentheses:

1. Who (author_____) you to sign this?
2. He tried to (min_____) his carelessness.
3. We (jeopard_____) our lives in that region.
4. We were (constr_____) to ask for his resignation.
5. He did not speak in an (intell_____) language.
6. We could not (det_____) him from going.
7. The company is beginning to (disint_____).
8. His attempt to reorganize proved (abor_____).
9. The last syllable in **respite** rhymes with (h_____).
10. Support of the team is in need of (invig_____).

Selection Exercise

Underscore the correct word in the parentheses:

1. Attorney Brown was (**debarred, disbarred**) for corrupt legaᴸ practice.
2. His (**urban, urbane**) manners were a great asset to him socially.
3. His age (**debarred, disbarred**) him from taking part in athletics.
4. The farmer's son finds it difficult to learn our (**urban, urbane**) customs.
5. (**Turbid, Turgid**) from the storm, the river had become a whirl pool (**turbid, turgid**) with sticks and sediment.

134

109

Words Often Confused

continuous   Uninterrupted; unbroken.

continual   Occurring in rapid and steady succession or at intervals.

Read aloud: There was a **continuous** murmur throughout his speech.

He slept **continuously** for seven hours.

There were **continual** interruptions during the baseball game.

He coughed **continually** during the meeting.

ingenious   Possessed of the faculty of invention; characterized by cleverness; adroit; shrewd.

ingenuous   Free from disguise; frank; candid.

Read aloud: He has invented an **ingenious** device for getting better mileage from automobiles.

Lincoln's **ingenious** remarks will live for ages.

Her **ingenuous** nature won her many friends.

He **ingenuously** confessed the part he took in the robbery.

exceptional   Not ordinary; uncommon; rare; better than the average.

exceptionable   Objectionable; open to censure.

Read aloud: He is a man of **exceptional** talents.

My son has manifested an **exceptional** aptitude for sports.

For his **exceptionable** conduct he was dismissed from office.

Such **exceptionable** remarks were unnecessary.

Practice

Place in sentences: **genius; ingenuity; ingénue; continuity.**

110

Verbs Ending in *ize*

eulogize   To extol in speech or writing; to praise; to write or speak in strong commendation of.
Read aloud: The speaker **eulogized** the work of the administration.
The aviator was **eulogized** for his great flight.

The noun, **eulogy**:
Read aloud: The **eulogy** at his funeral services was delivered by his intimate friend.

visualize   To form a mental picture of; to make visible; to conceive definitely.
Read aloud: We can still **visualize** him as he delivered his address.
Try to **visualize** the spelling of every difficult word.

harmonize   To bring into accord or agreement; to agree in sense or purport; to reconcile the apparent contradiction of.
Read aloud: It was obvious that their plans could not **harmonize**.
The colors in that room **harmonize** perfectly.
An attempt was made to **harmonize** their differences.

scrutinize   To examine closely; to inspect or observe with critical attention; to inspect carefully.
Read aloud: The auditor **scrutinized** the records of the bank.
The detective **scrutinized** each one who entered the place.

The noun, **scrutiny**:
Read aloud: No one could escape the **scrutiny** of the official.

Practice

1. How does **eulogy** differ from **elegy**?

2. Use in sentences: **visual**; **harmonious**.

111

Adjectives

venomous   Poisonous; spiteful; baneful; dipped in poison.
Read aloud: Such **venomous** statements were unnecessary.
He shot a **venomous** look at me.
The public feared his **venomous** pen.
He could not escape from the **venomous** darts of the editor.
Use in sentences: **venomous person; venomous remark;
venomous doctrine; venomous writer.**

relentless   Unyielding; mercilessly hard or harsh; without
pity; stern or persistent.
Read aloud: He was a **relentless** ruler.
Her attacks were **relentless.**
The **relentless** critic made many enemies.
Use in sentences: **relentless judge; relentless criticism;
relentless endeavor; relentless energy.**

ostensible   Apparent; pretended; professed; avowed.
Read aloud: His **ostensible** aim was to help those under him.
His **ostensible** reason for contributing to the campaign was
to help his party; his real reason was to obtain a political
job.
Her **ostensible** motive in coming was to sell me her home.
Those people are only **ostensibly** happy.

irrefutable   Incapable of proving false; that which cannot be
disproved.
(There are two correct pronunciations for this
word: ir ref′ u ta ble and ir″ re fut′ a ble.
The primary accent may be on the second or
on the third syllable.)
Read aloud: He presented an **irrefutable** argument against our
going to war.
She has an **irrefutable** claim to the property.

The adverb, **irrefutably:**
Read aloud: What was said was **irrefutably** true.

The noun, **refutation:**
Read aloud: The prisoner attempted no **refutation** of the
charge.

Practice

Use in sentences: **relent; ostentation.**

112

Adjectives Ending in *ious*

repetitious   Full of repetitions; tediously repeating.
(It is pronounced **rep e tish' us**.)
Read aloud: The speaker was very **repetitious**.
If I seem **repetitious** in giving these instructions, it is owing to my wish that you follow them carefully.

cautious   Careful; attentive to examine probable consequences of acts with a view to avoiding danger or trouble; prudent.
Read aloud: One should be **cautious** about his investments.
His answers were slow and **cautious**.
The general was too **cautious,** and as a result lost the battle.

disputatious   Inclined to dispute; apt to find fault or argue.
(It is pronounced **dis pu tay' shus**.)
Read aloud: I do not envy him his **disputatious** temper.
He is so **disputatious** that even his brothers are disinclined to converse with him.

expeditious   Quick; characterized by rapidity in action; speedy.
Read aloud: The work was done in an **expeditious** manner.
Expeditious action is necessary for the success of our plan.
No **expeditious** cure for the depression has yet been found.

surreptitious   Stealthy; secret; done without proper authority; made fraudulently.
(Pronounce it **sur ep tish' us**.)
Read aloud: There was a **surreptitious** removal of furniture from the house.
The paper commented upon the **surreptitious** acts of the suspect.

Practice

Write two synonyms for: **disputatious**; **expeditious**.

113

Words for Your Vocabulary

incapacitate   To render incapable or unfit; to disable; to dis-
qualify; to deprive of capacity or natural
power.
Read aloud: A broken finger **incapacitated** the golfer for the
tournament.
He knew that lack of schooling **incapacitated** him for such
work.
The teacher's fiery temper **incapacitated** her for classroom
instruction.

amplify   To enlarge, as by discussion; to treat copiously
by adding particulars, etc.; to expand; to ren-
der more extended.
Read aloud: He **amplified** his lecture with pictures.
I wish you would **amplify** your explanation of the trouble.

hazard (*v.*)   To risk; to put in danger of loss; to venture to
incur; to venture upon.
(This is one of the few two-syllable verb forms
which are accented on the first syllable: **haz'
ard.**)
Read aloud: In that country one fears to **hazard** an opinion.
I am willing to **hazard** my reputation on the success of this
patent.
The weak nation **hazarded** battle with the mighty one.

The noun, **haz' ard:**
Read aloud: He rescued the child at the **hazard** of his life.
We encountered many **hazards** in the jungle.
There are not many **hazards** on our golf course.

Practice

1.   Try to find two words that are derived from the same
roots as: **amplify**; **incapacitate.**

2.   Use in sentences: **hazardous**; **ample.**

114

Synonyms

obsolete   No longer in use; worn out; effaced.
obsolescent Going out of use; becoming out of date.
archaic   Old-fashioned or antiquated.
                 (Obsolete in the ordinary sense, but retained in special context or for special purposes.)

Read aloud: Picking cotton by hand on large plantations is now an **obsolete** custom.

The wearing of sailor straw hats by men seems to be an **obsolescent** style.

The words *saith, thou, erst, meseems,* and so forth, are considered **archaic** forms.

The following differentiation between **obsolete** and **archaic** is given by Fernald in his *English Synonyms and Antonyms* [1]:

"Some of the oldest or most ancient words are not obsolete, as *father, mother,* etc. A word is obsolete which has quite gone out of reputable use; a word is archaic which is falling out of reputable use, or, on the other hand, having been obsolete, is taken up tentatively by writers or speakers of influence so that it may perhaps regain its position as a living word."

practical   Having to do with action or practice rather than theory; useful; skillful from practice.

practicable   That may be done, or accomplished; capable of being used.

Read aloud: Aim to cultivate a **practical** vocabulary.

They have found a **practicable** method for combating diphtheria.

According to *Webster's New International Dictionary* (2nd ed.): "That is **practicable** (opposed to **impracticable**) which is capable of being accomplished; that is **practical** (opposed to **theoretical** and the like) which can actually be turned to account."

Practice

1. Give an antonym for **obsolete**.

2. Illustrate the use of the noun form of **practical**.

---

[1] Reprinted by permission of the publishers, Funk & Wagnalls Company.

Adjectives

timorous　　　Easily frightened; lacking in courage; shrinking; caused by timidity.

(The accent is on the first syllable: tim′ orous.)

Read aloud: Mr. Milquetoast is a **timorous** soul.

She had a **timorous** look.

He made a **timorous** appeal to the strikers.

Use in sentences: **timorous** laugh; **timorous** doubts; **timorous nature**; **timorous expression**.

inherent　　　Firmly or permanently contained; belonging by nature or settled habit.

(The accent must be placed on the second syllable: **inher′ ent.** Let the second syllable **her** rhyme with **dear**.)

Read aloud: In spite of reverses, he retained his **inherent** humor.

The desire to steal seemed to be **inherent** in him when he was a child.

predominant　　　Having ascendancy over others; superior, as in strength, influence, authority, or position; prevailing.

Read aloud: The **predominant** color was blue.

To acquire more territory was the dictator's **predominant** aspiration.

His **predominant** wish was that he would pass the examination.

Drink was his **predominant** weakness.

Use in sentences: **predominant** position; **predominant** asset; **predominant** demand; **predominant** ability.

116

Meaningful Expressions

sepulchral silence
sepulchral voice

> (**sepulchral**: Gloomy; funereal; dismal; suggesting a tomb.)
> (Accent the second syllable: **sepul′ chral.**)

Read aloud: **Sepulchral** silence pervaded the room as I entered.

The speaker's **sepulchral voice** lulled part of the audience to sleep.

salient characteristic
salient objection

> (**salient**: Standing out; easily seen; prominent; conspicuous.)
> (Be sure to pronounce this as a word of three and not two syllables. It is **say′ li ent**, not **sayl′ yent.**)

Read aloud: His **salient characteristic** was his honesty.

My **salient objection** to the plan is that it will require too much money.

vapid drink
vapid speech

> (**vapid**: Without much life or flavor; dull; spiritless; insipid; flat.)
> (The first syllable **vap** rhymes with **sap.**)

Read aloud: The host served a **vapid drink.**

I never listened to a more **vapid speech.**

onerous duties
onerous cares

> (**onerous**: Burdensome.)
> (The first syllable is **on**, not **o.**)

Read aloud: The college president found his **duties onerous.**

The **onerous cares** of the father were the cause of his untimely death.

Practice

1. Use in sentences: **salient** (*n.*); **onus.**

2. Write a synonym for: **vapid**; **sepulchral.**

Words for Your Vocabulary

ostentation   An unnecessary show; act of making an ambitious display; showing off; pretentious display.
Read aloud: There was little **ostentation** in his mode of life.
Ostentation is often a characteristic of vain people.

The adjective, **ostentatious:**
Read aloud: I dislike his **ostentatious** use of big words.
Her style was too **ostentatious** to be in good taste.

paucity   Fewness; small number; scarcity; smallness of quantity.
(It is pronounced: **po′ si ti**—the first vowel has the sound of the **o** in **orb.**)
Read aloud: He is a man with a **paucity** of ideas.
His **paucity** of words made him very self-conscious.
Paucity of funds shortened my vacation.

ascertain   To find out; to learn for a certainty; to get to know.
(It is pronounced **as er tane′.** Place the accent on the last syllable. Do not say **ascer′ tain.**)
Read aloud: We tried to **ascertain** the names of the boys who destroyed the property.
Kindly **ascertain** the cause of the trouble.

exigency   A case demanding prompt action or remedy; an emergency; urgent want.
(It is pronounced **ek′ si jen si.** Note that the first syllable is sounded **ek** and not **eg.**)
Read aloud: The police were ready for any **exigency.**
Whenever an **exigency** arises, try to be calm and cool.

The adjective, **exigent:**
Read aloud: We listened to the **exigent** request for food.
In **exigent** circumstances, he always played his part well.

Practice

1. Construct sentences with: **ostentatious; certainty.**
2. Write two synonyms for: **paucity; ostentation.**

Self-Check No. Thirteen

Matching Exercise

Select in Column II definitions for the words in Column I:

	I		II
	Verbs		
1.	scrutinize	*a.*	bring into accord
2.	visualize	*b.*	enlarge
3.	hazard	*c.*	examine closely
4.	harmonize	*d.*	extol in speech
5.	eulogize	*e.*	form a mental picture of
6.	incapacitate	*f.*	learn for certainty
7.	ascertain	*g.*	put in danger
8.	amplify	*h.*	render unfit
	Adjectives		
1.	relentless	*a.*	apparent
2.	ostentatious	*b.*	burdensome
3.	salient	*c.*	making unnecessary show
4.	venomous	*d.*	poisonous
5.	ingenuous	*e.*	prominent
6.	ostensible	*f.*	undisguised
7.	onerous	*g.*	unyielding

General Exercise

1. Have each adjective qualify two nouns: **timorous; disputatious.**

2. Construct sentences with: **paucity; ostentation.**

3. Define: **cautious; expeditious.**

4. What difference exists between **continual** and **continuous?**

5. To what word is **ingenious** related?

6. How does **exceptional** differ from **exceptionable?**

7. To what word is **coherent** related?

8. Give synonyms for: **archaic; apparent.**

9. What are the nouns related to: **sepulchral; scrutinize; eulogize?**

10. Use in sentences: **surreptitious; cautious.**

118

Words Often Confused

illegible   Not plain enough; incapable of being read; un-
        decipherable.
ineligible   Not qualified to be chosen or preferred; not suit-
        able.
        (Note the spelling of each of these words. Never
        say **ileligible**.)
   Read aloud: His handwriting is **illegible**.
   There was an **illegible** inscription on the tomb that was ex-
   cavated.
   A foreigner is **ineligible** for the Presidency.
   Tom is **ineligible** to play football because of his poor marks
   in English and mathematics.

aphasia   Loss of the power to use or understand speech.
amnesia   Loss of memory due to brain injury, shock, fever,
        etc.; also, a gap in one's memory.
        (Do not pronounce the first word **asphasia**.
        Note that one of these words pertains to loss
        of speech; the other, to loss of memory.)
   Read aloud: The **aphasia** victim has been in our city for more
   than a month.
   His **amnesia** was caused by shell shock during the World
   War.

Practice

1. Place in sentences: **illegal; legality; legalize; illicit;
eligibility; legibility.**

2. Construct sentences with: **legible; legal; eligible.**

145

119

Synonyms

alleviate	To lighten the force of; to make easier to be endured.
allay	To make quiet or put to rest; to relieve; to quell or calm.
assuage	To ease or lessen, as heat, pain, or grief.
mitigate	To moderate; to make less severe or painful, etc.; to soften or appease.

Read aloud: He tried to **alleviate** the financial burden of his parents.

The medicine seemed to **alleviate** the pain.

With a sickening heart she sought to **allay** the flux of blood.

The speech **allayed** the fears of the country.

We could not **allay** the public excitement.

He tried to **assuage** the widow's grief.

To **assuage** the sorrows of the poor was his mission in life.

The judge refused to **mitigate** the sentence.

A complete knowledge of the case **mitigated** the offense.

Webster's New International Dictionary (2nd ed.) gives the following differentiation:

"To **alleviate** is to lighten or render more tolerable; to **allay** is to abate or bring down from a state of tumult or excitement; to **assuage** is to quiet or render less violent; to **mitigate** is to soften or make milder."

Practice

1. Construct sentences with the noun forms of: **mitigate**; **alleviate**.

2. Use in sentences: **allay**; **mitigatory**.

Nouns Ending in *tion*

eruption
A bursting forth; a violent commotion; an outburst of passion, feeling, or the like.
(The first syllable is **e**, not **er**: **e rup′ shun**. The **e** is like the first **e** in **event**.)
Read aloud: There was an **eruption** of fire from the volcano.
What caused the **eruption** of feeling between them we shall never know.
It was one of his periodic **eruptions** of anger.
She is very sensitive because of her skin **eruption**.

exemption
Freedom from any charge, burden, etc., to which others are subject; immunity.
(Let the first syllable be pronounced **eg**, as: **eg zemp′ shun**.)
Read aloud: No **exemption** from military service was granted unless the case was a valid and deserving one.
Goods of foreign consuls receive an **exemption** from seizure.
The private schools did not receive **exemption** from taxes.

extirpation
Complete removal; total destruction; eradication.
(It is pronounced **ek ster pay′ shun**.)
Read aloud: The officials fought for an **extirpation** of gambling in the city.
We thought that the World War would bring about the **extirpation** of greed on the part of nations.

Practice
1. Use the verb form of: **exemption; extirpation.**
2. Write two synonyms for **extirpate.**

Adjectives Ending in *al*

rhetorical   According to rhetoric; using rhetoric; oratorical; intended especially for display.

(It is pronounced **re tor′ i kal.**)

Read aloud: He is more **rhetorical** than interesting.

The talk was more **rhetorical** than practical.

satirical   Containing ridicule or satire; given to the use of satire; severe in ridiculing men, manners, or things.

(The first i is sounded like the i in **pin: sa tir′ i cal.**)

Read aloud: It was a **satirical** essay on present-day manners.

He gave me a **satirical** look whenever I took the floor.

whimsical   Full of whims, fancy notions, or odd ideas; fanciful; odd.

(Do not pronounce it **wim′ si cal**; pronounce it as though it were spelled **hwim′ zi kal.**)

Read aloud: Poets are usually considered **whimsical** characters.

We found ourselves in a **whimsical** predicament.

His **whimsical** allusions have survived for years.

vernal   Pertaining to the spring; resembling the spring of the year in freshness and gentleness; hence, belonging to youth.

(It is pronounced **vur′ nal.**)

Read aloud: The **vernal** flowers did not live long.

There was a **vernal** freshness in his countenance.

Practice

1. Construct sentences with: **satirize; whim; satire.**

2. Give two noun forms of **rhetorical.**

122

Words for Your Vocabulary

impeach   To bring an accusation against; to call in question; to charge with a crime or misdemeanor; to bring or throw discredit upon.

Read aloud: The judge was **impeached** because of corrupt practice.

They **impeached** him for being a public nuisance.

Our motives were **impeached** by our adversaries.

The noun: **impeachment**:

Read aloud: We listened to the **impeachment** of his motives.

History records the **impeachment** of one United States President.

accrue   To come as a result of growth; to come by way of increase or advantage; to be added. (The pronunciation is **a kroo′**.)

Read aloud: Much good will **accrue** to you if you will devote a few minutes each day to word study.

Interest **accrues** to money left in a savings bank.

Many advantages will **accrue** to society as a result of the recent legislation.

perspective   The view in front; the effect of distance on the appearance of objects; the effect of the distance of events upon the mind; view of things in which they are in their right relations.

Read aloud: I take a different view of the matter now that I see it in **perspective**.

Becoming rich has changed his **perspective** of the poor.

It is necessary for us to look at things in their proper **perspective**.

Practice

1. Illustrate the difference in meaning between **perspective** and **prospective**.

2. Use in sentences: **impeachable; accrued** (*adj.*).

123

Pronunciation

digitalis   **digitay′ lis** or **digital′ is**
         A powerful heart stimulant.

No longer must the second syllable be pronounced **tay.** The form **tal** is now also recorded.

     Read aloud: The doctor prescribed **digitalis** for him.
         His heart did not respond to **digitalis.**

maestro   **mah e′ stro** or **mice′ tro**
         Master; teacher; master in any art, especially music; composer.

Radio announcers! Study well the pronunciation of this word. It has three syllables. *Webster's New International Dictionary* (2nd ed.) says that it is almost **my′ stro.** The second syllable **e** is sounded like the **e** in **get.** The first syllaable is **ma,** which rhymes with **pa.** The form **mice′ tro** is found in one or two dictionaries.

     Read aloud: Who is your favorite **maestro?**
         The **maestro** is ready to start the concert.

remuneration   (re mu″ ner a′ tion)
         Pay; reward; recompense.

The difficulty in this word is with the second syllable. It is **mu,** not **nu.** Too often we hear people pronounce it incorrectly: **re nu″ mer a′ tion.** Note that the primary accent is on the fourth syllable **a.**

     Read aloud: The **remuneration** he received from his writings was negligible.
     A knowledge that he had done his duty was ample **remuneration** for him.

Practice

Place in sentences: **enumerate; innumerable; remunerate; ıemunerative.**

124

Words for Your Vocabulary

abominable   Disgusting; very hateful; detestable; loathsome; disagreeable; unpleasant.

(The first syllable is **a : a bom′ i na ble.**)

Read aloud: He was severely punished for his **abominable** act.

His **abominable** language was disgusting.

Such **abominable** intentions must not be realized.

Last month we had **abominable** weather.

cadaverous   Having the qualities of a dead body; deathly pale; ghastly; gaunt; haggard.

(It is pronounced **ka dav′ er us.**)

Read aloud: He had a **cadaverous** look when he was released as a prisoner of war.

There was a **cadaverous** smell near the battlefield.

dilapidated   Falling to pieces; decayed; partly ruined by neglect; injured by bad usage.

Read aloud: We went through the **dilapidated** house.

He realizes that he has a **dilapidated** vocabulary.

A **dilapidated** wall bounds the rear of the property.

abeyance   Suspended activity; temporary inactivity or suppression; suspension.

(It is pronounced **a bay′ ance.**)

Read aloud: The answer to his question was kept in **abeyance** for weeks.

The names of the successful candidates will be held in **abeyance** for a month.

tractable   Capable of being easily led, taught, or controlled; easily managed.

Read aloud: The young man was no more **tractable** than a mule.

Children, as a rule, are very **tractable**.

He was too **tractable** for his own good.

Practice

Use in sentences: **abominate; intractable.**

125

Meaningful Expressions

interminable sufferings
interminable ride

> **interminable**: Endless; admitting no limit; wearisomely protracted.

Read aloud: We have read about the **interminable sufferings** of the soldiers in the trenches.

After what seemed like an **interminable ride,** we reached our destination.

diffuse writer
diffuse knowledge

> **diffuse**: Spread out; widespread; not concentrated or restrained; copious.
> (The last syllable in the adjectival form rhymes with **cluse** in **recluse.** The **z** sound is found only in the verb form. There it rhymes with **muse.**)

Read aloud: Shakespeare was a **diffuse** writer.

Our professor was a man of **diffuse knowledge.**

appreciable difference
appreciable supply

> **appreciable**: Large or material enough to be recognized or estimated.
> (Note that the third syllable is sounded **shi,** not **si.**)

Read aloud: There was an **appreciable difference** in the platforms of the two parties.

Our country now has an **appreciable supply** of radium.

astonishing speed
astonishing ease

Read aloud: The contractor completed the structure with **astonishing speed.**

My brother learned to speak French with **astonishing ease.**

fragile hopes
fragile vase

> **fragile**: Easily broken; delicate; frail; easily destroyed.
> (The **a** is sounded like the **a** in **cat,** not as in **care.**)

Practice

Construct sentences with: **diffuse** (*v.*); **infuse; suffuse.**

126

Words for Your Vocabulary

succinct   Expressed briefly and clearly; concise; terse; short.
(Note the pronunciation of the first and of the second syllable: **suk singkt'**.)
Read aloud: He gave a **succinct** account of his travels.
That author has a **succinct** style.

paramount   Above others; superior to all others; chief; pre-eminent; supreme.
Read aloud: What he said was of **paramount** importance.
This duty he considered **paramount** to all.

furtive   Done or obtained by stealth; sly; secret; stealthy.
Read aloud: There was something **furtive** in his actions.
The work was done in a **furtive** manner.

garrulous   Talking much, especially about trivial things; wordy; loquacious.
(The **a** is sounded like the **a** in **cat** and not like the **a** in **flare**.)
Read aloud: They soon tired of my **garrulous** friends.
Jack was a **garrulous** companion.

decry   To condemn; to make little of; to lessen the value by public condemnation; to clamor against.
(The accent must be placed on the last syllable: **decry'**.)
Read aloud: The teacher **decried** the use of slang in the class-room.
Many **decried** the $200-a-month pension plan.
The reformer **decried** alcoholic drinking in any form.

Practice

1. Use in sentences: **succinctly; garrulity.**

2. Write two synonyms for: **furtive; succinct.**

3. Give the antonyms of **furtive.**

Self-Check No. Fourteen

True and False Exercise

State which of the following statements are incorrect:

1. The **a** in **fragile** is short like the **a** in **cat**.
2. The third syllable in **appreciate** is pronounced **shi**.
3. **Succinct** is pronounced **suk singkt′**.
4. **Furtive** means "in vain, useless."
5. **Allay** is a synonym for **alloy**.
6. In the verb **diffuse**, the **s** has the sound of **z**.
7. The **a** in **digitalis** is like the **a** in **make**.
8. The primary accent in **remuneration** is on the **u**.
9. **Maestro** has three syllables.
10. **Ineligible** means "not qualified."

General Exercise

1. Write two meaningful expressions with the adjectives: **astonishing**; **interminable**.

2. How does **perspective** differ from **prospective**?

3. Use in sentences: **accrue**; **impeach**.

4. Name two synonyms for **mitigate**.

5. Where is the accent placed in the word **cadaverous**?

6. Consult a large dictionary for the derivation of **dilapidated**.

7. Have each adjective qualify two nouns: **tractable**; **rhetorical**.

8. Construct sentences with: **abeyance**; **garrulous**.

9. What are the verb forms of: **satirical**; **abominable**; **extirpation**?

10. Illustrate in sentences the meaning of: **eligible**; **aphasia**; **whimsical**.

Words Often Confused

frustrate	To prevent from attaining a purpose; to defeat.
fluster	To confuse; to muddle; to make hot and rosy, as with drinking.

(Frequently one hears the word **frustrate** used in place of **fluster**. The former has no connection with confusion or embarrassment.)

Read aloud: They endeavored to **frustrate** the will.

To try to **frustrate** his plans meant certain trouble.

The man was **flustered** when he learned that his trousers were torn.

I was **flustered** when I began to address the gathering.

contemptible	Worthy of contempt; deserving of scorn; despicable.
contemptuous	Expressing contempt or scorn.

(You can see by the definitions that **contemptible** pertains to receiving scorn, whereas **contemptuous** refers to giving scorn. One is taking, the other is giving, contempt.)

Read aloud: To steal from that poor man was a **contemptible** act.

He is considered the most **contemptible** person in our city.

There was no necessity for such **contemptuous** remarks.

Father gave me a **contemptuous** look when I tried to monopolize the conversation.

Practice

1. Use the noun form of **frustrate** in a sentence.

2. Construct sentences with: **frustrated plans; frustrated hopes; frustrated ambition.**

Words with the Prefix *trans*

There are many practical words that have for their prefix **trans**. This prefix means *across, over, through, beyond, or on the other side*. Note how one of these meanings is clear in each of the following words.

transport (*v.*)   To carry from one place to another; to carry away by strong feeling; to convey into banishment.

(The verb form is accented on the last syllable: **transport'**; the noun form, on the first syllable: **trans' port**.)

Read aloud: The troops were **transported** to New York.

He was **transported** with joy when he received word of his new position.

The noun form, **trans' port**:

Read aloud: The goods are now in **transport**.

She experienced **transports** of joy and sorrow during the last year.

transgress   To go beyond the limits set by; to pass over; to exceed.

(Accent the last syllable of this word: **transgress'**.)

Read aloud: He **transgressed** the laws of nature.

His language **transgressed** the bounds of an educated man.

That child has **transgressed** the limits of my patience.

transform   To change in form or appearance; to change in condition, nature, or character.

(Accent the last syllable: **transform'**.)

Read aloud: The vacation **transformed** him physically.

The caterpillar was **transformed** into a butterfly.

His new associations have **transformed** him from his morbid and sullen moods.

Practice

Use in sentences: **transmit; transcend; transparent; transcribe.**

129

Adjectives

immoderate   Too much; unreasonable; extreme; excessive.
Read aloud: I tried to caution him against **immoderate** drinking.
We could not meet their **immoderate** demands.
Such **immoderate** language was unwarranted.
Their **immoderate** mode of living exacted a heavy toll on their health and purse.
Use in sentences: **immoderate** tastes; **immoderate** desires; **immoderate** spending; **immoderate** laughter.

obdurate   Hardened in feelings or heart; unyielding; persistent; hardhearted; stubborn.
(The accent is placed on the first and not on the second syllable: **ob' durate**.)
Read aloud: He was an **obdurate** judge.
Mercy could not find a place in his **obdurate** heart.
The **obdurate** criminal refused to eat.
The people were **obdurate** in their demand that the leader resign.
Use in sentences: **obdurate** demands; **obdurate** conscience; **obdurate** disposition; **obdurate** foe.

expansive   Able to spread or expand; free; unrestrained; liberal in application.
Read aloud: We have read about the **expansive** force of heat.
He is a man of **expansive** wit.
The leader's power is very **expansive**.
The grounds about the clubhouse are **expansive**.
Use in sentences: **expansive** generosity; **expansive** site; **expansive** canvas; **expansive** outlay.

Practice

1. Construct sentences with: **immoderation**; **expansiveness**.

2. Pronounce **obdurate**.

130

Adjectives Ending in *able*

inevitable   Unavoidable; incapable of being shunned; sure
to happen.
(It is pronounced **in ev′ i ta ble**.)
Read aloud: If he continues to squander his money in this way,
his ruin is **inevitable**.
Death of the body is **inevitable**.
Failure was **inevitable** on account of his laziness.

impalpable   That which cannot be felt; intangible; that which
cannot be grasped by the mind.
(The pronunciation is **im pal′ pa ble**.)
Read aloud: There was an **impalpable** quality about the place
that made it most uninviting.
There is only an **impalpable** difference between the platforms of the two local parties.

ineffable   Incapable of being expressed in words; unutter-
able; indescribable.
(It is pronounced **in ef′ a ble**.)
Read aloud: He spoke of the **ineffable** mercy of God.
He referred to the **ineffable** beauty of the scene.
His disgust was **ineffable**.

indubitable   Not doubtful; too evident for doubt; unques-
tionable; certain.
(The second syllable is **du**, and not **dub**: **in du′
bi ta ble**.   The **u** is as in **cube**.)
Read aloud: His dishonesty was the **indubitable** cause of his
losing his good position.
The conclusion was **indubitable**.
They are **indubitably** mistaken.

Practice
Use in sentences: **inevitably; indubitably.**

131

Words for Your Vocabulary

voluble Easily rolling or turning; moving with ease and smoothness in utterance; of ready or rapid speech; glib.
(The pronunciation is **vol′ u ble**.)
Read aloud: Webster was a **voluble** speaker.
He has a **voluble** tongue.

retrieve To recover, as by study or an effort of memory; to regain; to make good; to repair, as a loss or damage.
Read aloud: They will endeavor to **retrieve** their financial losses.
It will be difficult to **retrieve** that mistake.

prolific Producing young or fruit; highly inventive; productive.
Read aloud: It is a **prolific** pear tree.
He has a **prolific** brain.

fictitious Feigned; imaginary; pretended; not real; not genuine.
Read aloud: Tom used a **fictitious** name.
It turned out to be a **fictitious** story.

strident Harsh-sounding; grating; shrill.
(The i is long: **stry′ dent**.)
Read aloud: He has a **strident** voice.
The **strident** sound of the foghorn awoke us.

Practice

1. How does **voluble** differ from **garrulous**?
2. Construct sentences with: **prolixity; volubility.**

132

Related Words *(lumin)*

Let us now direct our attention to a few words whose basic meaning pertains to *light*. We should strive to be able to employ these words both literally and figuratively.

luminous   Shining; reflecting or suggesting light; brilliant.
Read aloud: Here and there, through the breaches of the hills, the sunbeams made a great and **luminous** entry.
Stars are **luminous** bodies.
The attorney presented a **luminous** argument.

luminary   A body that gives light; one who is the source of light in the world in which he moves.
Read aloud: To the naked eye, the sun seems to be the largest **luminary** in the heavens.
Many intellectual **luminaries** were present at the conference.
Louis Pasteur was one of the **luminaries** in the field of science.

illuminate   To light up; to throw light upon; to enlighten.
Read aloud: Our streets are now **illuminated** by electric lights.
I shall try to **illuminate** this problem for you.

illumine   To light up; to enlighten.
Read aloud: A smile **illumined** the countenance of the urchin.
His speech was **illumined** by numerous anecdotes.

Practice

1. Construct sentences with: **illuminating; luminaries; nonluminous.**

2. Consult your dictionary for the root of **luminary.**

133

Words for Your Vocabulary

pernicious   Highly injurious or destructive in character; deadly; fatal; causing great harm or damage.
Read aloud: The gang had a **pernicious** influence upon him. Such **pernicious** doctrine should not be taught.

fabricate   To construct; to build; to form into a whole by uniting parts; to make up; to devise falsely.
(Note that the original meaning of this word is *to manufacture* and not, as many think, *to make up a lie*.)
Read aloud: The machine was **fabricated** abroad. He **fabricated** the story.

aberration   Act of wandering or going astray; deviation, especially from truth or a moral standard; wandering of the mind.
Read aloud: Their misdeeds were classified as **aberrations** of youth.
We soon realized that he was suffering from a mental **aberration**.

cognizant   Aware; having knowledge of.
(This word has two pronunciations: **kog′ ni zant** and **kon′ i zant**.)
Read aloud: The police were **cognizant** of the thief's hiding place.
He was **cognizant** of the fact that I had passed the test.

Practice

1. Construct sentences with: **recognizable; recognizance.**

2. Place **fabricate** in two original sentences.

3. Write two synonyms for **pernicious.**

4. Use in sentences: **fabrication; cognizance.**

134

Meaningful Expressions

legitimate demands
legitimate means
> *Read aloud:* The **demands** of the workers were **legitimate**.
> His place at the top was won by **legitimate means**.

detestable vices
detestable crime
> (**detestable**: Abominable; hateful; very odious.)
> *Read aloud:* He spoke of the **detestable vices** of his own people.
> For his **detestable crime**, he was sent to jail for life.

kindred propositions
kindred subjects
> (**kindred**: Belonging to the same family or race; related; being alike.)
> *Read aloud:* The two committees submitted **propositions** that were **kindred**.
> Latin and algebra can never be classified as **kindred subjects**.

irrevocably lost
irrevocably ruined
> (**irrevocably**: Unalterably; not able to be recalled or regained.)
> *Read aloud:* His fortune was **irrevocably lost** during the depression years.
> As a result of the act his reputation was **irrevocably ruined**.

perfunctory work
perfunctory advice
> (**perfunctory**: Done merely as a duty or for the sake of getting rid of the duty; marked by indifference. Accent the second syllable: **perfunc' tory**.)
> *Read aloud:* His **work** was always **perfunctory** and, as a result, not of much value.
> The **perfunctory advice** of the teacher invariably went unheeded.

135

Words for Your Vocabulary

circumvent   To get around; to gain advantage over by strat-
agem or deception; to cheat.
(The primary accent is on the last syllable:
cir″ cum vent′.)
Read aloud: His fame **circumvented** the country.
He tried to **circumvent** his opponent.
His attempt to **circumvent** the issue was an admission of
defeat.

pervade   To pass or go through; to penetrate; to pass or
flow through; to be diffused throughout.
(Accent the last syllable: **pervade′**.)
Read aloud: A flow of humor **pervaded** his talk.
The air was **pervaded** with the fragrance of roses.
A feeling of confidence **pervades** the whole assembly.

recant   To take back; to withdraw or renounce; to re-
pudiate formally and publicly.
(Accent the last syllable: **recant′**.)
Read aloud: He refused to **recant** what he said about Smith.
Punishment, however severe, could not make him **recant** his
religion.

The noun, **recantation**:
Read aloud: It was a forced **recantation**.
His refusal to make a **recantation** resulted in the loss of
his position.

efface   To rub out; to obliterate or destroy; to erase; to
do away with.
(Do not say **ee′ face**.   The first **e** has the sound
of the **e** in **get**.)
Read aloud: We could not **efface** the writing on the wall.
He tried to **efface** from his memory all thoughts of the accident.

Practice

Write two synonyms for: **recant**; **efface**.

Self-Check No. Fifteen

Completion Exercise

Verbs	*Adjectives*	
circumvent	cognizant	inevitable
frustrate	expansive	irrevocable
illuminate	fictitious	legitimate
illumine	flustered	perfunctory
pervade	impalpable	prolific
recant	indubitable	strident
retrieve	ineffable	voluble
transform		
transport		

Fill each blank with an appropriate word taken from the above list. Do not use the same word twice.

1. The speaker was too _____ to impress the audience.
2. He will endeavor to _____ his losses.
3. The work was done in a(n) _____ way.
4. It was _____ that he would lose the case.
5. He is now engaged in a(n) _____ business.
6. We were greatly _____ by his talk.
7. We were _____ by bus to his state.
8. There was a(n) _____ charm about the teacher.
9. Jones is a(n) _____ speaker.
10. She was not _____ of her brother's presence.
11. Shakespeare was a(n) _____ **writer.**
12. We could not _____ his question.
13. A(n) _____ voice tires the listener.
14. The loss of his fortune is _____.
15. A feeling of confidence _____ the country.

General Exercise

1. Write two synonyms for **recant,** each of which begins with **re.**

2. Give three words which contain the prefix **trans.**

3. Have each adjective qualify two nouns: **detestable; luminous.**

4. What is the sound of the first syllable in **heinous?**

5. Construct sentences with: **obdurate; immoderate.**

136

Words Often Confused

sensuous	Pertaining to the senses or sensible objects; characterized by sense impressions.
sensual	Devoted to the pleasures of sense and appetite; voluptuous; carnal; characterized by sense impressions; producing agreeable sense impressions.

(**Sensuous** is now used in a favorable or neutral sense; **sensual**, in a derogatory sense.)

Read aloud: This has been described as a **sensual** age.

The **sensual** pleasures of Henry VIII are mentioned by many historians.

He enjoyed the **sensuous** thrill of a plunge into the lake every morning.

"A poet is innocently **sensuous** when his mind permeates and illumines his senses; when they, on the other hand, muddy the mind, he becomes **sensual**."—Lowell.

salubrious	Favorable to health; conducive to well-being; beneficial; bright; warm.
lugubrious	Mournful; indicating sorrow, often ridiculously doleful.

Read aloud: We found the climate very **salubrious**.

It was a **salubrious** sky.

He always wears a **lugubrious** look.

The **lugubrious** howl of a wolf penetrated the silence of the night.

Practice

1. Use in two different sentences the verb **sense**.

2. Does the meaning of **salutary** resemble that of **salubrious**? Illustrate.

3. Write three words that are derived from the same root as **sensuous**.

Words with the Prefix *circum*

The prefix **circum** means *around or round about*.   Note its use in the following words.

circumference   The boundary line or perimeter of a circle.
> *Read aloud:* All points on the **circumference** are equidistant from the center.
> The **circumference** of the cyclone area included at least fifty towns.

circumstantial   Based on apparent facts; with many details.
> *Read aloud:* The evidence was entirely **circumstantial**.
> He rendered a **circumstantial** report of the meeting.

circumscribe   To enclose within certain limits; to restrict.
> *Read aloud:* **Circumscribe** those with a circle.
> The powers of the governor have been **circumscribed**.

circumspect   Cautious; prudent.
> (The accent is on the first syllable.)
> *Read aloud:* He is now a **circumspect** driver as a result of the accident of last year.
> We must be **circumspect** during this epidemic.

circumlocution   The use of many words where few are necessary.
> *Read aloud:* Many speakers should try to cure themselves of **circumlocution**.
> His explanation was vague because of his **circumlocution**.

Practice

1. Construct original sentences with: **circumnavigate; circumvention.**

2. Write three words whose last syllable is: **vent; scribe.**

3. Give two synonyms for: **circumvent; circumscribe.**

Adjectives

tangible   Capable of being touched; real; actual; definite.
Read aloud: Tangible benefits will result from his experiments.
There is a **tangible** difference between the two schemes.
They suffered **tangible** losses from being so headstrong.
Use in sentences: **tangible good; tangible result; tangible importance; tangible harm.**

salutary   Good for the health; wholesome; beneficial; conducive to a satisfactory outcome.
(The accent is on the first syllable: **sal′ u ter″ y.**)
Read aloud: The talk had a **salutary** effect upon the boy.
Salutary measures for helping the distressed were adopted at the meeting.
Use in sentences: **salutary exercise; salutary advice; salutary repentance; salutary change.**

acrimonious   Sharp or bitter in temper, language, or manner; caustic; stinging.
Read aloud: For his **acrimonious** language to the head of the college, he was expelled.
There was an **acrimonious** dispute between the two neighbors.

The noun, **acrimony**:
Read aloud: **Acrimony** rarely found a place in his criticism.

sagacious   Shrewd; wise in a keen, practical way.
(The second syllable, **ga,** is pronounced **gay.**)
Read aloud: The strikers disregarded his **sagacious** words.
He was a **sagacious** ruler.

Practice
Use in sentences: **intangible; acrimony.**

Verbs Ending in *ize*

familiarize
To make familiar or intimate; to accustom; to make to feel at ease; to make well known.
(The pronunciation of this word may be troublesome to some persons. It has four and not five syllables. Pronounce it **fa mil′ yer iz**, and not **fa mi′ li er ize**.)

Read aloud: One should **familiarize** himself with the dictionary.

The various speeches **familiarized** us with the meaning of democracy.

liberalize
To make, or become, liberal; to free or become or be free from narrow views or prejudices.

Read aloud: He endeavored to **liberalize** the minds of his people.

An attempt was made to **liberalize** our mode of instruction.

solemnize
To commemorate or observe with solemnity; to celebrate or honor in due fashion.

Read aloud: The marriage was **solemnized** with a nuptial mass.

They **solemnized** the rescue of their countrymen with prayer and fasting.

humanize
To make or become human; to give a human character or expression to; to soften; to make gentle by overcoming cruelty or rudeness.

Read aloud: The professor was a failure because of his inability to **humanize** his teaching.

The tyrant refused to **humanize** the laws of his kingdom.

capitalize
To convert into capital, or to use as capital; to furnish with capital; to provide capital for the operation of.

Read aloud: Jones has decided to **capitalize** on his athletic ability.

The government has **capitalized** the farmers.

Practice

Give the adjectival forms of: **capitalize**; **liberalize.**

140

Words for Your Vocabulary

beguile   To deceive; to cheat; to divert; to while away pleasantly.

Read aloud: We were **beguiled** into buying the property.

He **beguiled** time by reading.

Do not let anyone **beguile** you into thinking that vocabulary building is difficult.

necessitate   To make necessary or indispensable; to demand as a condition or consequence; to force; to compel.

Read aloud: His arrest for drunkenness **necessitated** his removal from office.

These extensive improvements will **necessitate** a slight increase in taxes.

The completion of his college course **necessitated** hard work and many sacrifices by his parents.

consecrate   To make sacred or holy; to dedicate, or devote something to some purpose; to hallow; to render sacred.

Read aloud: The church was **consecrated** last week.

He **consecrated** his life to the care of the lepers.

This is a custom **consecrated** by time.

spurious   Not genuine; false; sham; counterfeit.
(The first **u** is long, as in **cubc.**)

Read aloud: **Spurious** coins have been passed during the last week.

The document proved to be a **spurious** one.

They propagated **spurious** doctrines.

Practice

1. Have **spurious** qualify three nouns.

2. Write two synonyms for: **spurious; necessity.**

141

Synonyms

pertinacious Holding to an opinion, purpose, or design with obstinacy; resolute; often, perversely persistent.
    Rear aloud: They were **pertinacious** in their demands for shorter hours.
    Bulldogs are **pertinacious** fighters.

recalcitrant Kicking back; stubbornly rebellious; obstinate in defying constituted authority.
    Read aloud: There was a **recalcitrant** minority in the Senate.
    The leader was in a **recalcitrant** frame of mind.

callous Hardened in feeling, sensibility, etc.; unfeeling.
    Read aloud: The soap box orator seemed **callous** to ridicule.
    He possessed a **callous** heart.

inured Hardened; accustomed.
    (The second or last syllable **ured** should rhyme with **cured**. Accent the last syllable: **in ured′**.)
    Read aloud: The poor are **inured** to hardship.
    The invalid has become **inured** to pain.

Webster's New International Dictionary (2nd ed.) gives a clear explanation of the differences that exist among some of these synonyms:

"**Obstinate** implies persistent adherence, especially against persuasion or attack, to an opinion, purpose, or course.

"**Pertinacious** frequently connotes a persistence that is annoying or irksome.

"**Intractable** and **refractory** imply resistance to direction. **Intractable** more commonly refers to passive resistance; **refractory** to that which is active; as, **an intractable child** or **temper, a refractory pupil** or **animal.**

"**Recalcitrant** implies obstinate or violent reluctance to obey an order or follow a suggestion."

"**Obdurate** implies stubborn resistance to entreaty or softening influences.

"**Callous** both literally and figuratively implies a hardening or deadening of the sensibilities as a result of constant pressure or friction, or of repeated experience.

"**Inured** implies such toughening from use as lessens susceptibility to pain or inconvenience."

Words for Your Vocabulary

submerge
To put under water; to plunge; to bury or cover as with a fluid.

(The last syllable must be accented: **submerge'**.)

Read aloud: We watched him **submerge** his head in water.

He is **submerged** in debt.

dominate
To have a controlling power or commanding position over; to be the ruling force in; to control by strength or power.

Read aloud: The bully **dominated** the younger boys.

Fear **dominates** many speakers before they are introduced.

He **dominated** the meeting from the very moment that he arrived.

humility
Meekness; freedom from pride or arrogance; being humble in spirit.

Read aloud: He served his Lord with **humility** of mind.

A vein of **humility** could be detected in his speech.

Lincoln's **humility** was boundless.

elucidate
To make clear; to explain; to render intelligible by clear explanation.

(The first syllable is **e** and not **el**. It is pronounced like the **e** in **event**.)

Read aloud: I shall try to **elucidate** his theory.

The explanation did not **elucidate** the cause of the trouble.

magnify
To make larger; to enlarge; to exaggerate.

Read aloud: A **microscope** greatly **magnified** the object.

He seems to take delight in **magnifying** his trouble.

authenticate
To give authority to by proof; to establish the authorship of; to show to be valid or genuine.

Read aloud: The rumor about the leader's death has not been **authenticated**.

The document was **authenticated** by a seal.

143

Meaningful Expressions

unquestionably sound
unquestionably dangerous

> *Read aloud:* The monetary system of our government is **unquestionably sound.**
> He is an **unquestionably dangerous** person.

uncommonly learned
uncommonly low

> *Read aloud:* President Wilson was an **uncommonly learned** man.
> The price of clothes is **uncommonly low** this year.

strenuously assailed
strenuously objected

> (**strenuously**: In an active or energetic way.)
> *Read aloud:* They **strenuously assailed** every attempt to increase the tax rate.
> The child **strenuously objected** to going to bed.

rigidly adhered
rigidly followed

> *Read aloud:* They **rigidly adhered** to the customs of their ancestors.
> The executive **rigidly followed** the dictates of his conscience.

Practice

1. Have **strenuous** modify three nouns.

2. Use in sentences the adjectival form of: **unquestionably; rigidly.**

3. Write antonyms for: **strenuous; rigid.**

Words for Your Vocabulary

modify   To change somewhat the form or qualities; to alter somewhat; to make less severe; to qualify. (The first syllable **mod** rhymes with **cod: mod' i fye.**)

Read aloud: He refused to **modify** the terms of the contract. The punishment was somewhat **modified** by the judge. Adjectives may **modify** nouns.

rigorous   Very severe; harsh; strict; scrupulously accurate; exact.

Read aloud: We have just passed through a **rigorous** winter. He was a **rigorous** disciplinarian.

Use in sentences: **rigorous** demands; **rigorous** officer; **rigorous** rules; **rigorous** treatment.

imperative   Of the nature of a command; urgent; not to be avoided.

Read aloud: Aid to the needy is **imperative.**

It was his **imperative** duty to report the trouble.

It is **imperative** that I go to New York this week.

obsess   To beset; to haunt; to harass; to influence, as by a fixed idea, to an unreasonable degree. (The accent is on the last syllable: **obsess'.**)

Read aloud: Fear that he would be robbed so **obsessed** the miser that he became insane.

She is **obsessed** with the idea that her employer has a strong dislike for her.

Practice

1. Write two synonyms for **imperative.**

2. Use in sentences: **obsession; modification.**

Self-Check No. Sixteen

Matching Exercise

Find in Group II words to match the definitions in Group I.

I   II

Adjectives

1. Based on apparent facts.
2. Beneficial.
3. Capable of being touched.
4. Favorable to health.
5. Hardened.
6. Holding to a design.
7. Not genuine.

a. callous	j. spurious
b. circumspect	k. tangible
c. circumstantial	
d. inured	
e. lugubrious	
f. pertinacious	
g. salubrious	
h. salutary	
i. sensual	

Verbs

1. Beset.
2. Control by power.
3. Convert into capital.
4. Give a human expression to.
5. Make clear.
6. Make larger.
7. Make necessary.
8. Put under water.

a. beguile	j. obsess
b. capitalize	k. submerge
c. dominate	
d. elucidate	
e. humanize	
f. liberalize	
g. magnify	
h. modify	
i. necessitate	

General Exercise

1. Use in sentences: **consecrate; humility.**

2. Have each adjective qualify two nouns: **rigorous; acrimonious.**

3. What are the noun forms of: **modify; obsess?**

4. Use in sentences: **familiarize; lugubrious.**

5. Illustrate the meaning of: **callous; imperative.**

145

Words Often Confused

Though these two words closely resemble each other, there is a marked difference in their meanings.

aver To affirm with confidence; to declare in a positive manner, as in confidence of speaking the truth.

avert To turn aside, or away; to ward off, or prevent.

Read aloud: I **aver** that a reasonably large vocabulary is necessary for a good speaker.

That his failure is due to laziness I **aver** is the case.

The people could not **avert** the disaster.

The accident was **averted** by the quick thinking of the driver.

healthful Serving to promote health of body or mind; wholesome.

healthy Being in a state of health; enjoying health.

Read aloud: The country is a **healthful** place for the weak and sick.

That will prove **healthful** advice if received properly.

He returned from his long vacation strong and **healthy.**

To be **healthy,** you must eat **healthful** food.

Practice

1. To which of the above words is **aversion** related?
2. Write two antonyms for **healthful.**
3. Give a synonym for **aver.**
4. Construct a sentence with **avertible.**
5. Name three words whose last syllable is **vert.**

146

The Prefixes *ante* and *anti*

Though there is a marked similarity in appearance between these two prefixes, there is a difference in their meaning and pronunciation.

ante   Before, in regard to position, order, or time.
(It is pronounced **an′ te**. The **e** has the sound of the first **e** in **event**.)

anti   Opposite; against; instead of; opposed to; counter to.
(Care should be taken in the pronunciation of this word: it is **an′ ti**. The **i** has the sound of the **i** in **hit**. Do not pronounce the word **an′ tie**. That is the Latin form and has not yet been sanctioned by the makers of dictionaries.)

antedate   To date as of a time prior to that of execution; to precede in time.
Read aloud: He **antedated** the check.
Their rivalry **antedated** their college days.

antecedent
(adj.)   Going before; prior; preceding.
Read aloud: It was an event **antecedent** to his election.
What was the **antecedent** cause of his downfall?

antidote   A remedy to counteract the effects of poison; whatever tends to prevent mischievous results.
Read aloud: Milk or the white of an egg is an **antidote** for some poisons.
Activity is often an **antidote** for crime.

antisocial   Opposed to the principles on which society is based; averse to society.
Read aloud: Their organization is founded on **antisocial** principles.
Crime of any description is **antisocial**.

Practice

1. Use in sentences: **malevolent; malefactor; malediction; maldistribution.**

2. Write three words that contain the prefix: (*a*) **anti;** (*b*) **ante.**

Adjectives

adroit   Skillful; ingenious; exhibiting skill and readiness in avoiding or escaping difficulty.

(It is pronounced a droit'.)

Read aloud: His adroit use of the iron clubs won for him the golf championship.

He is noted for his adroit use of words.

Use in sentences: adroit reply; adroit management; adroit handling; adroit move.

depraved   Of very bad morals; characterized by debasement, corruption, or degeneration; perverted; corrupt.

(The a is long, as in gate: de prayvd'.)

Read aloud: Only a person with a depraved mind could commit such a crime.

The depraved criminal was placed in solitary confinement.

Use in sentences: depraved act; depraved conditions; depraved view; depraved look.

averse   Reluctant; unwilling; disinclined.

Read aloud: The hero was averse to flattery.

Richard is averse to going to college.

pungent   Causing a sharp sensation, as of the taste, smell, or feelings; piercing; acute, of speech, etc.; stinging or caustic.

(It is pronounced pun' jent.)

Read aloud: We tried to disprove his pungent statement.

He was much affected by the pungent editorial relative to his rule.

The pie had a pungent taste.

Practice

1. How does **dexterous** differ from **adroit**?

2. Construct sentences with: **aversion; depravity; adverse; adroitness.**

Adjectives Ending in *ious*

The following adjectives that end with the suffix **ious**, which means *full of or characterized by,* are formed from nouns ending in **y.**

harmonious   Marked by harmony or agreement in action or feeling; living in peace or friendship; free from discord.
Read aloud: It is a **harmonious** family.
The discussion was **harmonious.**
Her hat and dress were **harmonious.**

luxurious   Pertaining to luxury; supplied with the conditions of luxury; very comfortable.
(The first syllable may be pronounced **luks** or **lug,** thus: **luks u′ ri us,** or **lug zhoor′ i us.**)
Read aloud: They live in a **luxurious** home.
His life, though a **luxurious** one, must have been tedious at times.

parsimonious   Sparing in expenditure of money; frugal to excess; stingy; mean.
Read aloud: He acquired his wealth by being **parsimonious.**
Such a **parsimonious** life would not attract many people.
Only a **parsimonious** fare was given to the guests.

felonious   Malicious; traitorous; criminal; done with intent to commit a crime.
(Pronounce it **fe lo′ ni us.** The **e** is like the first **e** in **event.**)
Read aloud: The charge was **felonious** homicide.
He was sent to jail for **felonious** assault.

Practice

Construct sentences with: **harmony; parsimony; felony.**

149

Words for Your Vocabulary

oblivious   Forgetful; unmindful; unobservant; not conscious of.

(The first syllable is **ob**, not **o**: **ob liv′ i us**. The preposition is usually **of**.)

Read aloud: The pupils were **oblivious** of the teacher's presence in the rear of the room.

The conversation was so interesting that we were **oblivious** of the lateness of the hour.

Though suffering intense pain, he refused to be made **oblivious** by drugs.

The noun, **oblivion**:

Read aloud: The writings of that man have long ago dropped into **oblivion**.

The waters of **oblivion** have passed over the names of those heroes.

valorous   Courageous; brave; valiant.

(It is pronounced **val′ or us**.)

Read aloud: History will record the **valorous** deeds of our leader.

He made a **valorous** attempt to rescue the drowning child.

punctilious   Scrupulously exact in details or forms; very careful.

Read aloud: There was a **punctilious** observance of the holiday.

She was a **punctilious** hostess.

He is too **punctilious** in his use of words.

fragmentary   Disconnected; incomplete; made up of fragments.

Read aloud: The **fragmentary** remains of the automobile were taken to a dumping ground.

The victim gave only a **fragmentary** account of the shooting.

I am sure he will not be convicted, as the evidence at best was only **fragmentary**.

150

Related Words *(lud* or *lus)*

allusion   Act of referring directly or by suggestion; hint.
Read aloud: In Greek literature you will find many **allusions**
to mythology.
What was the purpose of the speaker's **allusion** to "a policy
of no foreign entanglements"?

elusive   Evasive; not easily comprehended; baffling.
Read aloud: Smith was the most **elusive** runner on the football
field.
The answer he gave was very **elusive**.

One may add to this family **elusion,** which means *act of
eluding; adroit escape, as by artifice; evasion.* Also, **elusiveness** and **elusory.**

illusion   An unreal or misleading image presented to the
vision; false impression; state of being deceived.
Read aloud: A mirage is an **illusion.**
Many are the **illusions** of youth about their future success
in the world.

illusive   Deceiving by false show; false; unreal.
Read aloud: He painted an **illusive** picture of what happened
at the meeting.
His ideas were as **illusive** as one's dreams of an earthly
paradise.

Practice

1. Construct sentences with: **delude; delusion; delusive;
allude; allusion; elude.**

2. What is the root of **delude?**

3. Let **delusive** modify two nouns.

151

Words for Your Vocabulary

estrange   To keep away, or keep at a distance; to divert
from its original purpose; to alienate the affec-
tions or confidence of.
(Accent the last syllable: **estrange′**.)
Read aloud: A quarrel over money has **estranged** the two
sisters.
Inability to obtain a position **estranged** him from the
party.

The adjective, **estranged**:
Read aloud: **Estranged** feelings exist between the two families.

spontaneity   Quality of being spontaneous; acting from na-
tive feeling or temperament without external
force.
(Note the sound of the third syllable: **ee**, and
also that there are five syllables in the word.)
Read aloud: His **spontaneity** of humor was a great possession.
We admired and praised the **spontaneity** of the child's
politeness.
What surprised us was the **spontaneity** of the revolution.

impunity   Freedom from punishment, bad consequences,
loss, or harm.
(Note that this word in itself means *without
punishment*. Therefore, do not use the expression **without impunity** unless you intend to use
a double negative.)
Read aloud: You cannot break the laws of nature with **impunity**.
He thought he could trespass upon private property with
impunity.
The subordinate thought that he could criticize the work of
his superiors with **impunity**.

Practice

1. Construct sentences with: **punitive; spontaneous.**

2. Let **estranged**, the adjective, qualify three nouns.

152

Meaningful Expressions

frantic effort
frantic appeal

        (**frantic**: Very much excited; wildly or uncontrollably moved; furious.)

Read aloud: A **frantic effort** was made to win the game in the last few minutes of play.

The mother of the condemned man made a **frantic appeal** to the governor for a reprieve of the sentence.

murky pool
murky cellar

        (**murky**: Dark; gloomy; obscure; dejected.)

Read aloud: The **pool** was so **murky** we could not see bottom.

The kidnapped child was kept in a **murky cellar**.

obvious defect
obvious meaning

        (**obvious**: Easily seen or understood; plain; evident. The first syllable is **ob** and is pronounced like the **ob** in oblong.)

Read aloud: The **obvious defect** of his plan was its impracticability.

The **meaning** of his departure from this country was **obvious** to all.

unabated efforts
unabated enthusiasm

        (**unabated**: Not growing less; continuing; not diminishing.)

Read aloud: The firemen continued with **unabated efforts** to fight the blaze.

They still speak of the victory with **unabated enthusiasm**.

Practice

1. Construct sentences with: **obviate**; **unabatable**.

2. Give two synonyms for: **murky**; **interminable**; **obvious**.

Words for Your Vocabulary

inveterate   Firmly established by age; not yielding to treatment; deep-rooted; confirmed in a habit or practice.
Read aloud: He has an **inveterate** dislike of study.
He is an **inveterate** drinker.
Wilson was an **inveterate** reader.

recoil   To draw back; to start to withdraw, as in horror, fear, or disgust; to spring back.
(The last syllable of this word must be accented: **recoil'**.)
Read aloud: The crowd **recoiled** at the scene of the hanging.
I **recoil** with fear when I think of my experiences on that night.
The wire **recoiled** when the tension was relaxed.

category   A class to which a certain assertion applies; a general division or classification; a class.
(Accent the first syllable: **cat' egory**.)
Read aloud: I would place him in the **category** of kind people.
He placed all words in two **categories**: those that are useful and those that are unnecessary.

idiotic   Very foolish; senseless; like an idiot.
Read aloud: It was an **idiotic** thing for him to attempt to escape from that prison.
Pay no attention to his **idiotic** demands.

vagary   Wandering of the thoughts; a departure from the expected or normal course; an eccentric procedure, notion, or action.
(Pronounce this word **va gay' ry** or **va gare' ry**. The first **a** is like the **a** in **sofa**.)
Read aloud: The idea that we would have moving sidewalks was another **vagary** of his.
The gambler attributed his losses to the **vagaries** of the cards.
The lecturer referred to the **vagaries** of the child.

Self-Check No. Seventeen

Completion Exercise

adroit	felonious	oblivious
averse	frantic	obvious
avid	idiotic	parsimonious
callous	illusive	punctilious
depraved	inveterate	spontaneous
elusive	lamentable	valorous

Fill each blank with an appropriate word taken from the above list:

1. He has a(n) _____ dislike for Latin.
2. It was _____ that he would fail in business.
3. Do not be deceived by his _____ promises.
4. We were totally _____ of the time.
5. The judge ruled that the attack was made with _____ intent.
6. The leader made a(n) _____ move.
7. We realized that we had made a(n) _____ mistake.
8. To refuse the education appropriation would be merely _____.
9. She is very _____ about the kind of clothes she wears
10. Brown has a(n) _____ style of writing.
11. His good will is always _____ and never forced.
12. She made a(n) _____ appeal for help.
13. His _____ deeds are known by all.
14. The people had sunk to a(n) _____ condition.
15. Her remarks were of a(n) _____ nature.

General Exercise

1. Pronounce: **anti; ante.**
2. Write two expressions with: **adroit; unabated.**
3. Where is the accent placed in **lamentable?**
4. Use in sentences: **fragmentary; impunity.**
5. Give the noun form of: **frantic; averse; oblivious.**

154

Related Words *(cred)*

incredulous Not disposed to believe or admit what is related as true; skeptical.

(Do not confound this word with **incredible.** The third syllable **du** is pronounced like the **du** in **verdure.**)

Read aloud: We found him too **incredulous** to do business with.

The **incredulous** politician soon found himself in a labyrinth of trouble.

credulity Belief or readiness of belief.

(The second syllable is pronounced **dew.**)

Read aloud: The orator spoke of the sanguine **credulity** of youth.

It was easy to gain Mr. *X*'s support because of his **credulity.**

creditable Suitable; respectable; reputable; worthy of judicious praise.

Read aloud: Our football team made a **creditable** showing against the championship eleven.

The conduct of the class was **creditable.**

discreditable Injurious to reputation; disgraceful; disreputable.

(Note that the prefix is **dis** and not **in.**)

Read aloud: For his **discreditable** act he was severely punished.

The horse ran a **discreditable** race.

Practice

1. From what root word are the above words taken?

2. Use in sentences: **credible; credence.**

3. What is the meaning of **credentials?**

4. Give the noun form of: **creditable; discreditable.**

155

Words with Prefix *omni*

This prefix is derived from the Latin word **omnis,** which means *all.* When it is used as an adjective or a noun, it denotes that some specified action or quality has unrestricted or universal range.

omnivorous Eating or, figuratively, devouring everything; especially, eating both animal and vegetable food. (The accent is on the second syllable: **om niv′ o rus.**)

 Read aloud: His brother is an **omnivorous** reader.

 Man is an **omnivorous** animal.

omnipotent All-powerful; almighty; able in every respect and for every work. (Be sure to accent the second syllable: **om nip′ o tent.** Never say **om nip po′ tent.**)

 Read aloud: God is **omnipotent.**

 The dictator thinks he is an **omnipotent** ruler.

omnipresent Present in all places at the same time; ubiquitous.
 Read aloud: The employer seemed to be **omnipresent.**

 In the stricter meaning of this word, only God is **omnipresent.**

Ubiquitous has the meaning of being present or turning up, especially unexpectedly, in many places.

omniscient Having universal knowledge; knowing all things; infinitely wise. (It is pronounced **om nish′ ent.**)

 Read aloud: We cannot deceive **omniscient** God.

 Young pupils look upon their teachers as **omniscient** beings.

Practice

1. What is an **omnibus?**

2. Give the noun form of: **omnipotent; omniscient.**

3. How does the accent in **omnipotent** differ from the accent in **omnipresent?**

156

Adjectives

nocturnal Occurring in the night; moving about at night. (The accent is on the second syllable: **nok tur′ nal.**)

Read aloud: His brother accompanies him on his **nocturnal** walks.

The owl is a **nocturnal** bird.

Gerald was in the habit of making **nocturnal** trips to the lake.

Use in sentences: **nocturnal** darkness; **nocturnal** quiet; **nocturnal** recreation; **nocturnal** walks.

incarnate Invested with flesh or bodily nature; personified; enshrined; impersonated. (Be sure that the accent is on the second and not on the first syllable: **in kar′ nate.** The last syllable is pronounced like the last syllable in **senate.**)

Read aloud: He is a villain **incarnate.**

The lady was grace **incarnate.**

The noun: **incarnation** (Accent the third syllable.):

Read aloud: He was the **incarnation** of embarrassment when confronted with the question.

expedient Useful; helping to attain some end; practical and efficient; advantageous. (It is pronounced **ex pee′ di ent.**)

Read aloud: It was considered **expedient** to replace some of the men.

He presented an **expedient** solution of the problem.

What is **expedient** may not always be considered right.

Practice

1. Is **expedient** always a synonym for **just** or **honest?** Prove your answer.

2. Use **expediency** in a sentence.

157

Adjectives Ending in *able*

inexplicable   Mysterious; incapable of being explained, interpreted, or accounted for.

(This word is mispronounced very frequently. Stress the second syllable and there will be no difficulty in pronouncing it correctly: **in eks' pli ka ble.** It is never **in eks plik' a ble.**)

Read aloud: The crime will ever remain, I believe, an **inexplicable** mystery.

The disaster was caused by one of Nature's **inexplicable** acts.

The adverb, **inex' plicably:**

Read aloud: He was **inexplicably** mean to his aged parents.

impeccable   Not liable to sin; exempt from the possibility of wrongdoing; of things, free from fault or error.

Read aloud: Man is far from being an **impeccable** creature.

He has left office with an **impeccable** record.

The language he uses is **impeccable.**

malleable   That can be extended or shaped by beating with a hammer; adaptable; yielding.

Read aloud: Most metals are **malleable**; steel and cast iron are the outstanding exceptions.

That student seems to lack a **malleable** mind.

The agitator found his audience in a very **malleable** mood.

Practice

1. Use in sentences: **peccable; explicable.**

2. Pronounce: **despicable; inapplicable.**

158

Words for Your Vocabulary

subjugate To subdue; to conquer; to make subservient; to bring under the yoke of power or government.

Read aloud: The tribe was totally **subjugated** by the white men.

If one cannot **subjugate** his lust for money, his pleasures in life will be few.

consummate (*v.*) To complete; to raise to the highest point or degree; to finish; to achieve; to fulfill.

(Though there are still a few authorities which permit two pronunciations for this verb, there is now a tendency to restrict it to **con′ summate,** the last syllable rhyming with **late.** The other form is **consum′ ate,** the last syllable being pronounced **it.**)

Read aloud: The work will be **consummated** next week.

His happiness was **consummated** when he received a substantial scholarship for college.

One of the last words of our Lord was, "It is now **consummated.**"

consummate (*adj.*) Complete; perfect; of the highest quality; carried to the utmost degree.

(The adjectival form has only one pronunciation, as though spelled **kon sum′ it.**)

Read aloud: He has manifested **consummate** skill as an engineer.

The young man was a **consummate** pianist.

She was a woman of **consummate** virtue.

Practice

1. Use in sentences: **conjugate; consume.**
2. What are the noun forms of: **consummate; subjugate?**
3. Give two synonyms for the adjective **consummate.**

Pronunciation

orgy   (or′ jy)
        Drunken revelry; carousal; a manifestation of excessive indulgence in some predilection.

Note that the **g** is sounded like the **g** in **ginger**, and not like the **g** in **girl**.

    Read aloud: The police were summoned to quell the **orgy**.
    The banquet witnessed an **orgy** of speechmaking.

philatelist   (philat′ elist)
        One who collects or studies postage stamps.

Note that the accent is on the second syllable, which rhymes with **cat**.

    Read aloud: The **philatelist** has a valuable collection of stamps.
    A **philatelist** derives much pleasure from his hobby.

bestial   (best′ yul *or* bes′ chul)
        "Brutal; vile; beastly."

The first syllable should be pronounced **best** or **bes**. Do not pronounce it **beast**.

    Read aloud: He was disliked because of his **bestial** nature.
    The invaders were later punished for their **bestial** acts.

Practice

1. Pronounce: **philately**; **philatelic**.
2. Give an antonym for **oral**.
3. What letter in **orgy** is often mispronounced?
4. Write the pronunciation of: **choral**; **oracular**.

Words for Your Vocabulary

diffident   Wanting confidence in oneself; distrustful of one's own powers; timid; shy.
Read aloud: He was a very **diffident** person.
A **diffident** feeling gripped him as he approached the executive.

The noun, **diffidence**:
Read aloud: His **diffidence** was a great obstacle to him.

complicity   State of being an accomplice; participation in guilt; partnership in wrongdoing.
Read aloud: For his **complicity** in the crime, he was sentenced to five years in jail.
Buying stolen goods is **complicity** in theft.

petulant   Quick to take offense; peevish; irritable; subject to little fits of bad temper; irritable over trifles.
(Pronounce it **pet′ chu lant″**.)
Read aloud: The child became **petulant** when asked to do anything.
We did not expect such a **petulant** answer.

inhibition   Act of prohibiting; restraint; embargo.
(The accent is on the third syllable: **in hi bish′ un**.)
Read aloud: Parents should not place too many **inhibitions** on their children.
He tried to overcome his **inhibitions**.

expunge   To blot out, as with a pen; to strike out; to obliterate; to destroy; to wipe out.
(Accent the second syllable: **eks punj′**.)
Read aloud: We were not permitted to **expunge** one paragraph from the story.
The offense was **expunged**.
Certain statements had to be **expunged**.

Practice

Illustrate in sentences the meaning of: **inhibit; diffidence**.

Verbs Ending in *ize*

deputize   To appoint as deputy; to act as deputy.
Read aloud: He was **deputized** to inform the employees of their increase in pay.
We **deputized** him to arrange a meeting with the executives.

fraternize   To associate in a brotherly way; to have brotherly feelings; to be friendly.
(The first syllable is **frat**, which should rhyme with **brat**.)
Read aloud: Some of our soldiers **fraternized** with the enemy during a lull in the fighting.
Young boys should not **fraternize** with anyone of doubtful reputation.

modernize   To render modern; to cause to conform to recent or present usage, style, method, etc.
Read aloud: Some teachers do not **modernize** their work in the classroom.
Plans have been drawn to **modernize** our office building.

crystallize   To form with definite shape; to cause to assume a fixed and definite form.
Read aloud: Public opinion has begun to **crystallize** for our candidate.
Belief that he has committed the crime has **crystallized**.

mobilize   To render movable; to put into movement or circulation; to assemble and put in readiness for active service in war.
Read aloud: He **mobilized** all his strength for the approaching struggle.
All the converging railroad lines were **mobilized** for the transportation of troops.

Practice

Construct sentences with: **crystal** (*adj.*); **fraternal**; **modernistic**.

Words for Your Vocabulary

advocate (*v.*) To plead in favor of; to recommend publicly; to support.

(The last syllable of this word, **ate**, rhymes with **fate**: ad' vo kate.)

Read aloud: He **advocates** an eight-hour working day.

The president of the college **advocated** the teaching of vocabulary building to all classes.

The noun, **advocate**: this form is pronounced differently from the verb. The last syllable **ate** is like the **ate** in **senate**.

Read aloud: He is an **advocate** of a bigger navy for our country.

We are staunch **advocates** of fair play.

Another related noun is **advocacy**. It is pronounced **ad' vo ka sy.**

Read aloud: His **advocacy** of prohibition cost him his re-election to office.

assail To attack with violence or vehemence; to assault; to molest.

Read aloud: He **assailed** the burglar with blows.

The crowd **assailed** the umpire with fiery expressions because of his decision.

resurrect To raise from the dead; to disinter; to bring to view again that which was forgotten or lost.

Read aloud: They tried to **resurrect** some of the old blue laws.

Where did he **resurrect** that 1900 automobile?

Practice

1. Use in sentences: **advocacy; insurrection.**

2. Give the meaning of: **vocal; vocalize; advocate** (*n.*)**; vocation.**

3. Pronounce the noun **advocate.**

Self-Check No. Eighteen

True and False Exercise

Which of the following statements are not true?

1. The root of the word **credit** is **credo.**
2. An antonym for **creditable** is **incredible.**
3. **Expedient** means "what is always honest and just."
4. The first syllable of **oral** is **o,** not **or.**
5. We must always accent the first syllable of **incarnate.**
6. The accent in the adjective **consummate** is on the second syllable.
7. **Complicity** is a synonym for **wrongdoing.**
8. **Diffidence** is a synonym for **scepticism.**
9. **Fraternize** is related to the word **fraternal.**
10. In the word **inexplicable,** the accent is always on the second syllable.

General Exercise

1. Have each adjective qualify two nouns: **expedient; incarnate.**

2. Construct sentences with: **diffident; expunge; nocturnal.**

3. Use in sentences the noun form of: **omniscient; consummate; advocate; expedient.**

4. Give synonyms for: **faultless; irritable; assail.**

5. How is the second syllable of **credulity** pronounced?

163

Synonyms

impending Overhanging; about to fall or happen.
imminent Threatening to occur immediately; near at hand.
threatening Indicating a menace or some approaching evil. (A **threatening** evil or peril may happen soon or late, but there is always the hope of averting it; an **impending** evil is one that is almost sure to happen—it may be near or remote; **imminent** is the strongest of the three terms, and applies to that danger or evil which threatens to happen immediately or is on the point of happening.)

Read aloud: **Impending** bankruptcy shattered his nerves.

The dark clouds told us a storm was **impending.**

As the threat of war became more **imminent,** all the nations rushed to strengthen their defenses.

You saved me from **imminent** death at the hands of the bandits.

Sharp lightning indicated that a severe storm was **imminent.**

A **threatening** letter was sent by the kidnapper.

He shot a **threatening** glance at me when I disclosed his corrupt dealings.

foretell *Webster's New International Dictionary* (2nd
predict ed.) discriminates thus between these words:
prophesy "Foretell and predict are frequently interchange-
forecast able; but **predict** is now commonly used when inference from facts (rather than occult processes) is involved. **Prophesy** connotes inspired or mysterious knowledge, or great assurance of prediction. **Forecast** connotes conjecture rather than inference."

Practice

1. Use in sentences: **prophesy; predict.**
2. Write three words whose last syllable is **pend.**

164

Words with the Prefix *trans*

transmute   To change from one nature or form into another; to transform; to convert.

(The accent is placed on the last syllable: trans- mute'.)

Read aloud: The news of the victory **transmuted** our grief to joy.

Water power can be **transmuted** into electrical power.

He thought he could **transmute** a base metal into gold.

transfix   To pierce through as with a pointed weapon; to impale; to hold fixed or motionless.

(The last syllable receives the accent: transfix'.)

Read aloud: The sword **transfixed** his shoulder.

He was **transfixed** with astonishment.

When he received word of his son's accident, he remained **transfixed** for a minute.

transfuse   To pour from one vessel into another; to diffuse itself through; to instill.

(Accent the last syllable: transfuse'.)

Read aloud: They **transfused** blood from the father to the son.

The speaker could **transfuse** his beliefs and enthusiasm to the minds of the audience.

The air was **transfused** with sunshine.

translucent   Shining or glowing through; that penetrates so as to illumine; partly transparent; letting light through.

(The accent should be placed on the second syllable: translu' cent.)

Read aloud: **Translucent** brick walls are no longer a novelty in houses.

The curtains are **translucent**.

165

Adjectives

accessible Easy to reach; approachable; open to the influ-
ence of.
(The second syllable receives the accent: **access′
ible.**)
Read aloud: The executive is not an **accessible** person.
Kindly put the comb and brush in a more **accessible** place.
He has a mind **accessible** to reason.

comprehensible Understandable; capable of being understood; in-
telligible; conceivable.
Read aloud: Everything is **comprehensible** to God.
His English was scarcely **comprehensible**.
He has an amount of worldly goods that is scarcely **com-
prehensible**.

inimitable Not capable of being imitated; matchless; beyond
imitation.
(Place the accent on the second syllable: **in im′ i
ta ble.**)
Read aloud: Lincoln was a man of **inimitable** humor.
The style of Shakespeare is **inimitable**.
She has an **inimitable** smile.

alienable That may be taken away or withdrawn.
(This word now has two correct pronunciations.
It may be a word of four or of five syllables:
ail′ yen a ble, or **a′ li en a ble.**)
Read aloud: The depression taught us that wealth is **alienable.**
Knowledge is not **alienable**.
Happiness and health are **alienable** possessions of man.

Practice

Use in sentences: **comprehend; alienate; accessory; com-
prehension.**

166

Adjectives Ending in *ible*

We often experience considerable difficulty in spelling words that end in **ible**. We may not be sure whether they should end in **able** or **ible**. If you will remember this rule, it may remove considerable doubt from your mind about the correct form: if the corresponding noun ends in **sion, tion,** or **ition,** the suffix will be **ible**. This rule does not cover all **ible** words.

EXAMPLES: division   divisible

                  destruction   destructible

                  audition   audible

Try to make these adjectives an integral part of your speaking vocabulary.

reducible   Capable of being reduced, of being changed to another form, of bringing to a different condition.

Read aloud: What he said was **reducible** to this, namely, that we are on the verge of another war.

My finances are now at an **irreducible** minimum.

destructible   Capable of being destroyed; liable to destruction.

Read aloud: This glassware is not **destructible**.

Everything **destructible** was safely put away.

permissible   Allowable; that may be permitted; admissible.

Read aloud: It was not **permissible** to visit the flood area.

They are only the **permissible** shortcomings of youngsters.

admissible   Worthy to be admitted; that may be allowed or conceded; allowable.

Read aloud: Only **admissible** testimony was recorded.

Visitors were not **admissibie** after 6 p. m.

Practice

1. What is the difference in meaning between **admission** and **admittance?**

2. Construct sentences with: **reduction; destructive; inadmissible.**

167

Words for Your Vocabulary

dynamic Characterized by energy or effective action; active; potent; forceful.
(The second syllable receives the accent: **dye nam′ ik.**)
Read aloud: He has a **dynamic** personality.
We listened to a **dynamic** speech on the monetary system.
A more **dynamic** leader could not be found.

culminate To reach the highest point, as of power, rank, etc.
(Pronounce this word **kul′ mi nate.**)
Read aloud: His disregard for law and order **culminated** in his downfall.
Such honest and effective work will surely **culminate** in promotion.

remunerate To reward; to pay for work, services, trouble, etc.; to compensate; to recompense.
(We frequently hear this incorrectly pronounced **re nu′ mer ate.** The second syllable is **mu** and not **nu.** The pronunciation is **re mu′ ner ate.**)
Read aloud: The man was well **remunerated** for his services.
An increase in salary will **remunerate** him for his faithful work.

The adjective, **remunerative:**
Read aloud: He did not find writing very **remunerative.**
Baseball playing is one of our most **remunerative** sports.

Practice

1. Write a synonym and an antonym for **dynamic.**

2. Construct sentences with: **remuneration; culmination.**

168

Nouns Ending in *tion*

perdition   Utter loss; eternal death; total destruction.
(It is pronounced **per dish′ un.**)
Read aloud: Many reformers think that the young people of today are fast going to **perdition**.
The preacher said the soul of an unrepentant sinner suffers **perdition** after the death of the body.

requisition (*n.*) An act of requiring; a formal written demand; that which is required.
(The pronunciation is **rek″ wi zish′ un.**)
Read aloud: I have forwarded a **requisition** for more food for the soldiers.

Do not confuse this word with **requisite,** which means "that which is required or necessary; something indispensable." It is pronounced **rek′ wi zit.**
Read aloud: The **requisites** for that position are numerous and rigid.

The verb, **requisition:**
Read aloud: The general **requisitioned** horses for his troops.

coalition   A combination or union; union into a body, as of separate bodies or parts; alliance.
(It is pronounced **ko a lish′ un.**)
Read aloud: There has been a **coalition** of two of the minor parties.
A **coalition** of those nations will make them a very powerful group.

rendition   Act or result of rendering; surrender; translation.
Read aloud: His **rendition** of that operatic piece was excellent.
The merchant demanded a **rendition** of the furniture for lack of payment.
The class play will be a **rendition** of one of Shakespeare's works.

Words for Your Vocabulary

perceptible   Capable of being perceived; discernible; capable of being known by the senses.
Read aloud: Your nervousness was not **perceptible**.
There was a **perceptible** breeze on the veranda.
There is a **perceptible** difference in business circles this year.

The noun, **perception**:
Read aloud: He is endowed with wonderful mathematical **perception**.
The people seem to have no **perception** of what is right or wrong.

emulate   To try to equal or excel; to imitate with a view to equal or to outdo; to rival.
Read aloud: She is trying to **emulate** the splendid college record of her sister.
Try to **emulate** those who are industrious and honest.

capitulate   To surrender on certain terms or conditions (usually drawn up under certain heads).
(It is pronounced **ka pi' chu late**.)
Read aloud: The strikers, having been out of work for a month, were ready to **capitulate**.
The leader was ready to **capitulate** on condition that the soldiers be allowed to go home.

fetish (*n.*)   Any object of special or unreasoning devotion; irrational reverence; a thing supposed to have magic powers.
(There are two correct pronunciations for this word: **fee' tish** and **fet' ish**. The first syllable of the second form should rhyme with **get**.)
Read aloud: He made a **fetish** of card playing.
Do not make a **fetish** of big words.

Practice

Use in sentences: **capitulation; emulation.**

Meaningful Expressions

unremitting toil
unremitting efforts

> (**unremitting**: Incessant; persevering.)
> *Read aloud:* His was a life of **unremitting toil.**
> The speakers praised the **unremitting efforts** of the missionaries to convert the pagans.

hollow sympathy
hollow victory

> *Read aloud:* Her **hollow sympathy** was of small help in his hour of need.
> Though he won by a margin of a few votes, it proved to be a **hollow victory,** as he was not permitted to take his seat in the Senate.

grinding poverty
grinding despotism

> *Read aloud:* **Grinding poverty** prevented his attendance at any social functions.
> The people began to complain of the **grinding despotism** that made them no better than slaves.

defiant attitude
defiant way

> (**defiant**: Bold; insolent; disobedient.)
> *Read aloud:* His **defiant attitude** to the new employer resulted in immediate trouble between the two.
> For answering his father in such a **defiant way,** he was severely punished.

accustomed clearness
accustomed severity

> *Read aloud:* The lawyer answered his adversary with his **accustomed clearness.**
> He eventually treated his employees with his **accustomed severity.**

caustic remarks
caustic rebuke

> (**caustic**: Burning, severe, sharp.)
> *Read aloud:* You should have taken exception to his **caustic remarks.**
> The chauffeur received a **caustic rebuke** for damaging the car.

Practice

Write two synonyms for: **caustic; unremitting.**

Words for Your Vocabulary

captious
    Hard to please; fault-finding; eager to object; apt to catch one.
    (This is a two-syllable word: **kap′ shus**.)
Read aloud: The **captious** critic was very unpopular.
It was difficult to tolerate the **captious** child.
Many **captious** questions were asked.

caption
    The heading of a chapter, section, page, or article.
Read aloud: What is the **caption** of the story?
The **caption** was in a modern type.

fuse
    To join together by melting; to blend; to unite; to melt.
    (The **s** has the sound of **z**: **fuz**. The word should rhyme with the verb **use**.)
Read aloud: The two large industrial plants have **fused**.
Intense heat was applied in order to **fuse** the metals.

The noun, **fusion**:
Read aloud: In this country we have a **fusion** of nationalities.
Some educators are opposed to the **fusion** of the bright with the dull pupils.

retract
    To withdraw; to recall; to take back; to disavow.
    (Accent the last syllable: **retract′**.)
Read aloud: She refused to **retract** what she said.
He threatened to **retract** the offer.

The noun, **retraction**:
Read aloud: The teacher insisted that the pupil make a **retraction**.
The man who falsely accused me of stealing has made a **retraction** of the charge.

Practice

Construct sentences with these synonyms for **retract**: **recant; rescind.**

Self-Check No. Nineteen

Matching Exercise

Nouns	*Verbs*	*Adjectives*
coalition	advocate	admissible
culmination	capitulate	caustic
destruction	consummate	defiant
fetish	emulate	dynamic
perdition	expunge	imminent
prophecy	prophesy	inimitable
rendition	retract	permissible
requisition	transmute	threatening

Fill the blanks with the proper words from the list.

1. Unexcused lateness was not _____.
2. His _____ skill is missed on the football field.
3. He felt like one condemned to _____.
4. The _____ of his school career was his graduation with highest honors.
5. She _____ one of the moving picture stars.
6. He thought he could _____ coming events.
7. His _____ attitude toward the authorities led to suspicion and arrest.
8. A _____ nature made him a leader.
9. He is ready to _____ his harsh statement.
10. He handed in a _____ for the prisoner.

General Exercise

1. Give the noun form of **alienable**.

2. Have the word **captious** qualify two nouns.

3. Give synonyms for: **threatening**; **prophecy**.

4. Give two words related to the noun **requisition**.

5. Pronounce: **inimitable**; **alienable**.

6. Define: **recapitulate**; **precipitate**; **commute**.

7. Give the antonym of: **translucent**; **comprehensible**; **accessible**.

8. Give a synonym for: **discernible**; **rival** (*v*.).

9. Define: **accession**; **recession**; **concession**.

10. Give two words related to: **rendition**; **predict**.

Figurative Expressions

Figurative Expressions

The Simile

Of the different figures of speech, the most common and at the same time the most effective are the simile and metaphor. The simile is defined as "a figure of speech by which one thing, action, or relation is likened or explicitly compared in one or more aspects, often with **as** or **like,** to something of different kind or quality." In other words, it is an expression of likeness or comparison introduced by such terms as **like** and **as.** EXAMPLE: "He runs like a deer." Here, the speed is likened to the swiftness of a deer. The simile is **like a deer.**

The Metaphor

The *metaphor* is often called an *implied simile.* It is a comparison without the use of the words **like, as,** and so forth. It is attributing to a person or thing characteristics that belong to something else. "He runs like a deer on the football field" is a simile because the comparison is expressed. "He is a deer on the football field" is a metaphor because the swiftness, a characteristic of a deer, is attributed to him.

EXAMPLES:
The general and his men were a stone wall during the battle.
His temper leaped beyond his control.
He shot an angry look at me.

Words and phrases also may be used in a metaphorical sense. Thus, **golden hair, fiery temper,** and **pearly teeth** employ figurative adjectives.

Suggestions for Metaphoric Writing

Select the important word and ascertain what some of its characteristics or meanings are. Take the simple words **dig** and **fetter. Dig** means "to turn up the soil with a spade; also, to seek light by turning up the soil." "He will **dig** a trench" is the literal use of the verb. "We shall **dig** more deeply into the study of words" is the figurative use of the verb.

Fetter means "to chain down or to bind." "The hands and feet of the slaves were **fettered**" is the literal use of **fetter.** "He is **fettered** to the belief that he has a malignant disease" is the figurative use.

Nouns may be used in like manner. Take the words **current, volley,** and **veil.** The expressions **current of crime, volley of abuse,** and **veil of sarcasm** are all figurative uses.

Importance of Metaphors

Metaphors, if not too numerous and if not forced, enliven, clarify, and add force to one's speech, whether written or oral. Aristotle centuries ago said, "The most important thing to a writer or speaker is to have the power of metaphors."

Figurative Uses

bars of restraint
bars of slavery
> *Read aloud:* The subjects tried to batter down the **bars of restraint** placed on them by their imperious rulers.
> The **bars of slavery** were removed by the Emancipation Proclamation.
> *Use in sentences:* **bars of enmity; bars of fear.**

The verb **bar** is used figuratively also:
> *Read aloud:* His scant purse **barred** him from taking a vacation.

beam of happiness
beam of satisfaction
> *Read aloud:* Never was a **beam of happiness** able to penetrate his melancholy life.
> A **beam of satisfaction** lighted his countenance.
> *Use in sentences:* **beam of comfort; beam of enthusiasm.**

As a verb:
> *Read aloud:* The players **beamed** with confidence as they started the game.

shower of sympathy
shower of condemnation
> *Read aloud:* A **shower of sympathy** descended upon those who were left destitute by the tornado.
> He could not escape the **shower of condemnation** that followed his speech.
> *Use in sentences:* **shower of abuse; shower of praise.**

As a verb:
> *Read aloud:* They **showered** him with gifts and money.

dust of guilt
dust of defeat

Read aloud: Although he was acquitted of the crime, still the **dust of guilt** clung to his name for many years.

We could not remove from their minds the **dust of last year's defeat.**

Use in sentences: **dust of greed; dust of toil.**

As a verb:

Read aloud: We **dusted off our memories** by a fifteen-minute weekly review.

glow of pride
glow of kindness

Read aloud: A **glow of pride** spread over his mother's face while he spoke.

For a moment there was a **glow of kindness** in his manner, usually so rough.

Use in sentences: **glow of friendship; glow of health.**

As a verb:

Read aloud: His **heart glowed** with love for all his people.

flood of light
flood of remorse

Read aloud: A **flood of light** entered the room when I raised the shade.

He was overcome by a **flood of remorse** for his treacherous deed.

Use in sentences: **flood of bank notes; flood of hatred.**

As a verb:

Read aloud: We **flooded** our representative at Washington with letters pertaining to the proposed legislation.

harvest of success
harvest of souls

Read aloud: He reaped a **harvest of success** as a result of his diligence and perseverance.

He brought to his church a **harvest of souls** through his missionary work.

Use in sentences: **harvest of regrets; harvest of debts.**

As a verb:

Read aloud: They are now **harvesting the rewards** of their venture.

legacy of words
legacy of happy remembrances

Read aloud: He received a **legacy of words** from his systematic study of the dictionary.

Father left us a **legacy of happy remembrances.**

Use in sentences: **legacy of noble thoughts; legacy of ill temper.**

209

mask of dishonesty
mask of charity
> *Read aloud:* He was forced to remove his **mask of dishonesty.**
> The culprit collected much money under the **mask of charity.**
>
> *Use in sentences:* **mask of meanness; mask of innocence.**

As a verb:
> *Read aloud:* He tried **to mask the real purpose** of his visit.

note of confidence
note of sarcasm
> *Read aloud:* The speech sounded a **note of confidence** among the salesmen.
> We detected a **note of sarcasm** in his words.

robe of determination
robe of conceit
> *Read aloud:* He was forced to don the **robe of determination** in order to complete the work.
> Were she to take off her **robe of conceit,** she would be more popular with the students.
>
> *Use in sentences:* **robe of leniency; robe of humility.**

As a verb:
> *Read aloud:* Her **face was robed** in smiles when her father met her.

atmosphere of crime
atmosphere of learning
> *Read aloud:* The urchin was brought up in an **atmosphere of crime.**
> In such an **atmosphere of learning** it was easy for us to study and concentrate.
>
> *Use in sentences:* **atmosphere of happiness; atmosphere of sorrow.**

shackles of greed
shackles of convention
> *Read aloud:* **Shackles of greed** prevented his enjoying life like other men.
> Too frequently are we bound by the **shackles of convention.**
>
> *Use in sentences:* **shackles of timidity; shackles of regret.**

As a verb:
> *Read aloud:* He was so **shackled by debt** that he became discouraged and ambitionless.

blast of misfortune
blast of bitterness
> *Read aloud:* His nerves could not withstand another **blast of misfortune.**

210

That **blast of bitterness** changed the course of his life.
Use in sentences: **blast of adversity; blast of temper.**

As a verb:
> *Read aloud:* The depression **blasted his hopes** of ever becoming wealthy again.

depths of despair
depths of knowledge
> *Read aloud:* He was in the **depths of despair** when I found him in New York.
>
> It is impossible to plumb the **depths of his knowledge.**
>
> *Use in sentences:* **depths of feeling; depths of winter.**

school of experience
school of adversity
> *Read aloud:* Lessons learned in the **school of experience** are lasting and profitable.
>
> He was brought up in the **school of adversity,** and as a result his outlook upon life was dark.
>
> *Use in sentences:* **school of hard knocks; school of optimism.**

As a verb:
> *Read aloud:* Our soldiers were well **schooled in the science of war.**

breath of honesty
breath of peace
> *Read aloud:* One could detect a **breath of honesty** in his every word.
>
> We have not enjoyed a **breath of peace** for many years.
>
> *Use in sentences:* **breath of sadness; breath of contempt.**

searchlight of truth
searchlight of investigation
> *Read aloud:* The **searchlight of truth** was turned upon his record.
>
> No one was able to escape the rays of their **searchlight of investigation.**
>
> *Use in sentences:* **searchlight of happiness; searchlight of success.**

veil of silence
veil of doubt
> *Read aloud:* The **veil of silence** was never broken by him.
>
> A **veil of doubt** still surrounds him.
>
> *Use in sentences:* **veil of night; veil of obscurity.**

As a verb:
> *Read aloud:* He endeavored **to veil his talk** with optimism

211

chill of remorse
chill of defeat
> *Read aloud:* A **chill of remorse** ran through his mind when
> he realized what he had done.
> It was the first **chill of defeat** that the candidate had felt.
> *Use in sentences:* **chill of adversity**; **chill of anxiety**.

As a verb:
> *Read aloud:* The results of the straw vote **chilled our hopes**
> of success.

warmth of friendship
warmth of love
> *Read aloud:* One felt the **warmth of friendship** whenever he
> was present.
> The **warmth of his love** dispelled all feelings of jealousy
> and revenge.
> *Use in sentences:* **warmth of piety**; **warmth of response**.

web of lies
web of destiny
> *Read aloud:* The witness was easily caught in his own **web
> of lies.**
> Napoleon spun his own **web of destiny**, which was defeat.
> *Use in sentences:* **web of deceit**; **web of contradictions**.

As a verb:
> *Read aloud:* **His acts were webbed** with trickery and debauch-
> ery.

avenue to fame
avenue of ruin
> *Read aloud:* His latest book has placed him on the **avenue to
> fame.**
> Many youths of today are racing along the **avenue of ruin**.
> *Use in sentences:* **avenue of comfort**; **avenue of success**.

valley of peace
valley of disappointment
> *Read aloud:* Once again we found ourselves in the **valley of
> peace.**
> Countless thousands dwelt in the **valley of disappointment**
> during the depression years.
> *Use in sentences:* **valley of remorse**; **valley of forgetfulness**.

spark of discord
spark of animation
> *Read aloud:* Only another **spark of discord** was necessary to
> produce a conflagration among the European nations.
> His speech lacked the **spark of animation**.
> *Use in sentences:* **spark of wit**; **spark of enthusiasm**.

anchor of debt
anchor of grief

> *Read aloud:* A heavy **anchor of debt** forbade him the freedom that others enjoyed.
>
> She seemed at all times to be oppressed and held down by the **anchor of grief.**
>
> *Use in sentences:* **anchor of laziness; anchor of servitude.**

As a verb:

> *Read aloud:* They seemed **anchored to the belief** that our government was wrong.

pendulum of prosperity
pendulum of public opinion

> *Read aloud:* The **pendulum of prosperity** is not swinging in our direction.
>
> Those in authority carefully study the **pendulum of public opinion.**
>
> *Use in sentences:* **pendulum of hope; pendulum of activity.**

abyss of ignorance
abyss of misery

> *Read aloud:* The people were in an **abyss of ignorance** in regard to the monetary system.
>
> Many families found themselves in an **abyss of misery** as a result of hard times.
>
> *Use in sentences:* **abyss of crime; abyss of sorrow.**

Some Spelling Rules

Some Spelling Rules

RULE 1:

   a. Words ending in final **e** usually drop the final **e** before a syllable beginning with a vowel: for example, **ride, riding.** Exceptions are found in compounds taking the suffix **able,** for example, **marriageable, serviceable,** *etc.*

   b. If the added syllable begins with a consonant, the final **e** is usually retained: for example, **manage, management; peace, peaceful.** (**Judgment** and **acknowledgment** may be written with the e before **ment.**)

   c. If the word ends in double **e,** both **e**'s are retained before a vowel or a consonant: for example, **agree, agreeing, agreement.**

RULE 2:

   Monosyllables and words accented on the last syllable and ending in a single consonant preceded by a single vowel double the final consonant before a suffix beginning with a vowel: for example, **run, running; begin, beginning.**

RULE 3:

   a. Words ending in **y** preceded by a consonant change **y** to i before a suffix not beginning with **i:** for example, **enemy, enemies; family, families; ally, allies.**

   b. If final **y** is preceded by a vowel, the **y** is retained before a suffix: for example, **valley, valleys; alloy, alloys.**

RULE 4:

   Monosyllables ending in double **f, l,** or **s** following a single vowel generally retain the final consonant when a suffix is added: *e.g.,* **will, willful** (the preferred spelling).

RULE 5 (**Ei** and **ie** combinations):

   a. When these are sounded like **e, ei** is used after **c,** and **ie** after any other consonants: for example, **receive, believe, grieve,** *etc.*

   (*Note:* There are a few exceptions to this rule. Among these are: **leisure, seize, neither,** *etc.*)

   b. When these are sounded like **ay, ei** is used: *e.g.,* **reign, veil,** *etc.*

   c. When these are sounded like long **i, ie** is generally used: *e.g.,* **die, lie,** *etc.*

(*Note:* Exceptions are certain words ending in **ght**, such as **height, sleight,** *etc.,* and some foreign terms, such as **eiderdown.**)

d. When these are sounded like short **e** or **i**, **ei** is generally used: as **heifer, foreign,** *etc.*

e. When these vowels are pronounced separately, **ie** is commonly used: *e.g.,* **alien, salient.** *etc.*

RULES FOR USE OF THE HYPHEN

The hyphen is used:

1. When **ex-** precedes titles: *e.g.,* **ex-president,** *etc.*
2. In spelled-out numbers below one hundred, when these consist of more than one word: *e.g.,* **twenty-two,** *etc.*
3. When a numeral adjective precedes **-rate** or **-hand**: *e.g.,* **second-hand,** *etc.*
4. Between the numerator and the denominator of spelled-out fractions: *e.g.,* **three-fourths,** *etc.*
5. When certain adjectival expressions are compounded: *e.g.,* **fair-haired,** *etc.*

RULES FOR FORMING THE PLURALS OF NOUNS

1. The regular rule for forming the plurals of most nouns is to add **s** to the singular. If the final letter of the singular does not unite in sound with **s** (as in the case of **x, z, ch, s,** and the like), add **es:**

boy	boys	box	boxes
horse	horses	church	churches

2. If a noun ends in **y** preceded by a consonant, the plural is formed by changing the **y** to **i** and adding **es:**

history	histories	daisy	daisies
city	cities	memory	memories

3*a.* If a noun ends in **o** preceded by a consonant, add **es** to form the plural:

veto	vetoes	hero	heroes
tomato	tomatoes	potato	potatoes

(Some exceptions to this rule are: **pianos, solos, cantos.**)

b. To nouns ending in **o** preceded by a vowel, add **s:**

folio	folios	cameo	cameos

4. If a noun ends in **f** or **fe,** change the **f** or **fe** to **ves** to form the plural:

knife	knives	calf	calves

Some exceptions are:

dwarf	dwarfs	proof	proofs
safe	safes	scarf	scarfs
chief	chiefs	roof	roofs

5. Irregular plurals are:

man	men	woman	women
mouse	mice	goose	geese
foot	feet	cherub	cherubim [1]

6. In forming compound plurals, care should be taken to distinguish the principal word, as it does not always occupy the same position. Usually only the principal word is changed to the plural form, as in:

son-in-law	sons-in-law	court-martial	courts-martial
man-of-war	men-of-war	fellow-servant	fellow-servants

The following, however, change in both parts:

Knight-Templar	Knights-Templars
man-servant	men-servants

7. Words ending in **ful** form their plurals by adding **s**:

spoonful	spoonfuls	pailful	pailfuls
mouthful	mouthfuls	handful	handfuls

8. Letters of the alphabet, numbers, and mathematical signs form their plurals by adding **'s**:

r's　　a's　　4's　　9's　　+'s　　x's

9. The following words have the same form in the singular and in the plural:

means	sheep	mackerel	series
athletics	ethics	wages	deer
politics	bellows	species	hose

10. Some words have two plurals whose meanings are different:

brother	brothers	*(of a family)*	brethren	*(in a church)*
head	heads	*(of bodies)*	head	*(of cattle)*
fish	fishes	*(used separately)*	fish	*(used collectively)*
cannon	cannons	*(used separately)*	cannon	*(used collectively)*

---

[1] Or: **cherubs.**

11*a.* Plurals of foreign words. We have retained in our language many words whose singular and plural forms are the same as in the foreign language from which they were taken. Some, however, have been Anglicized in their plural forms.

Singular	Plural	Singular Definition
thesis	theses	Essay.
datum	data	Fact.
basis	bases	Foundation.
crisis	crises	Turning point.
stratum	strata	Layer.
alumnus	alumni	Male graduate.
alumna	alumnae	Female graduate.
ellipsis	ellipses	Omission.
hypothesis	hypotheses	Supposition.
analysis	analyses	Examination.
bacillus	bacilli	Germ.
diagnosis	diagnoses	Determination.

b. The following words have both the foreign plural form and an English plural formed by adding **s**:

phenomenon	phenomenons	or	phenomena
automaton	automatons	or	automata
criterion	criterions	or	criteria
cherub	cherubs	or	cherubim

Self-Check No. Twenty

General Exercise

A. Write three words that end in **-ceive.**

B. Write two words in which **ei** has the sound of **ay.**

C. What rule applies to each of the following words?

ceiling	mischief	sieve	leisure
neighbor	besiege	transient	daily
sleigh	achieve	foreign	height
forfeit	weigh	handkerchief	acknowledgment

D. The following words are exceptions to what spelling rule?

pianos	proofs	hoofs
dwarfs	scarfs	handkerchiefs
solos	daily	

E. Can you find three mistakes in these sentences?

1. It is difficult to understand the phenomenas of nature.
2. I took two spoonsful of sugar.
3. We heard weird sounds.
4. The seige lasted a month.

F. State what rule, if any, applies to each of these words:

brief	niece	sieve	mischief
siege	pierce	friend	believe
priest	shriek	achieve	cashier
field	yield	frieze	receipt
rein	veil	weird	kerchief
fruit	reign	either	conceit
weigh	neigh	leisure	height
sleigh	eighty	deceive	forfeit
aggrieve	glacier	weight	seizure
foreign	chief	fierce	skein
unveil	besiege	reprieve	seignior
fiend	lieu	relief	feint
ancient	frontier	prairie	transient
deficient	mien	alien	seismic (sīs'-)
quotient	patient	wield	lieutenant
series	heir	adieu	convenient

G. Which of the following words are exceptions to the rule?

convenient	(—yent)	Adapted to one's comfort; handy.
inalienable	(—al'yen a b'l)	That cannot be taken away.
leisure	(lee'zhur)	Spare time at one's disposal.
seize	(seez)	To take possession of by force; to grasp.
counterfeit	(—fit)	Spurious; bogus; not genuine.
grievous	(greev'us)	Causing sadness; painful; oppressive.
financier	(fin an seer')	One skilled in money transactions.
proficient	(—shent)	Thoroughly qualified; skillful.
sovereign (*n.*)	(sov'er in)	Ruler, such as a king, emperor, or potentate.

Application Exercise

Tell the spelling rule that applies to each of the words in bold type in the following sentences. If the word is an exception to a rule, state the rule.

1. The goods were **shipped** to Europe.
2. He **offered** his services to us.
3. Many **solos** were heard during the evening.
4. We did not start the **argument**.
5. Name three **heroes** of the Civil War.
6. The boys **studied** all afternoon.
7. While we were **studying,** he took a walk.
8. **Relief** was sent to the flood victims.
9. He could not be **deceived** so easily.
10. **Twenty-five** students passed the examination.
11. He failed to **seize** the opportunity.
12. There were many **dwarfs** in the show.
13. The children were **well-bred.**
14. It was an **excusable** act.
15. We could not **inveigle** him into buying the lot.
16. There was not much **sleighing** last winter.
17. **Neither** of the boys **received** his own hat.
18. The **alumnae** returned for the reunion.
19. Many **theses** were written by the class.
20. The **data** were presented by the executive.
21. This country has experienced many financial **crises.**
22. A rose was **pinned** on his lapel.
23. They are **pining** for their lost fortune.
24. We carried many **pailfuls** of water.
25. Have you sent an **acknowledgment** of the invitation?

Prefixes and Suffixes

Prefixes and Suffixes

LATIN PREFIXES

A letter or syllable added at the beginning of a word to change its meaning is called a **prefix**.

Some Latin prefixes and their meanings follow:

Prefix	Meaning	Illustration
a, ab	From, away.	avert, abstain
ad, af, at	To.	adhere, affix, attain
ante	Before.	antedate, antemeridian
circum	Around, about.	circumference, circumnavigate
con, cor	With, together.	convene, correspond
contra, counter	Against.	contradict, counteract
de	From, down.	descend, debase
di	Apart.	divert, divorce
dis	Not.	disagree, dissuade
e, ex	Out of, from.	eject, exit
extra	Beyond.	extravagance
in, im, ir, il	Not.	inappropriate, impossible, irresponsible, illegal
per	Through.	permeate, percolate
post	After.	posterity, postpone
pre	Before.	predict, precede
pro	For, forth.	pronoun, procession
re	Back, again.	recall, revive
sub, subter	Under.	subordinate, subterfuge
super	Over, above.	superintendent, supervise
trans, tra	Across, beyond.	transport, traverse

GREEK PREFIXES

Inasmuch as the majority of words in the English language are derived from both Latin and Greek, it will be well to examine the more important Greek prefixes. Having compared the prefixes taken from the two languages, you will readily see that a greater supply is obtained from the Latin.

Prefix	Meaning	Illustration
a, an	Without.	atheist, anarchist
ambi, amphi	Both, around.	ambidextrous, amphitheater
ana	Through.	analysis
ant, anti	Against.	antonym, antipathy

225

Prefix	*Meaning*	*Illustration*
apo	From.	apology
cata	Down.	catacomb, cataract
dia	Through.	diameter, diagnosis
epi	Upon.	epitaph, epigram
hyper	Above, over.	hypercritical, hyperbole
hypo	Under.	hypodermic
meta	Beyond.	metaphysical
mono	One.	monologue, monocle
para	Similar.	parable, parody
peri	Around.	perimeter
poly	Many.	polysyllable, polygon
syn	With.	syndicate, synonym

SUFFIXES

A suffix is a letter or syllable added to the end of a word or word-root to change its meaning. Examples are:

able, ible	That may be; worthy of: movable, blamable, lovable, usable.
ac, al, ial	Pertaining to; of the nature of: cardiac, national, facial.
ance, ence	State of being: abundance, difference, obedience.
ant, ent	One who; that which: servant, student, superintendent.
er, or	One who: teacher, instructor, sailor.
ful	Full of: hopeful, helpful, skillful.
ish	Having the quality of: boorish, mannish, boyish.
ity	The quality of: servility, humility, ability.
ive	One who; that which: executive, sensitive.
logy	Science, theory, etc., of: physiology, theology.
less	Without: voiceless, restless, sleepless.
ly	Like: manly, cheerfully, lazily.
ness	State of: goodness, loneliness, holiness.
ous	Full of: anxious, joyous, ridiculous.
ry	State of: rivalry, discovery, ministry.

Self-Check No. Twenty-One

Exercise on Latin Prefixes

Give the root word and the Latin prefix of these words, and show how the prefix affects the meaning:

subscribe	subterranean	innumerable
concurrence	demoralize	perambulate
disappoint	commiserate	translucent
supernatural	excommunicate	extraordinary

Exercise on Greek Prefixes

Give the root word and the Greek prefix of each of these words, and tell how the prefix affects the meaning:

amphibian	paraphrase	synchronize
epidemic	synthetic	polychrome
monosyllable	periscope	hypersensitive
hypocrite	antiseptic	polytechnic

Dictionary Exercise

Explain the prefixes and suffixes in:

boyhood	nominee	interpose	posterity
stenography	interfere	circumvent	theorize
playwright	microscope	prehistoric	sophomore
		autograph	

General Exercise on Prefixes and Suffixes

Explain the prefixes and suffixes in:

transgress	digestible	illogical	antecedent
postpone	deduce	fateful	anteroom
anagram	biology	perspire	abduct
claimant	eatable	anarchy	detract
preface	reiterate	subordinate	antedate
antidote	efface	transpose	superficial
	abdicate	theology	

Sixty-Eight Vocabulary Quizzes

Sixty-Eight Vocabulary Quizzes

1—Selection Quiz

(Based on page 15.)

Select the proper word in parentheses:

1. The building in which the state legislature meets is called the (**capital, capitol**).
2. My supply of (**stationary, stationery**) is becoming very low.
3. The members of the (**counsel, council**) will meet once a month.
4. His motives proved him to be a man of high (**principle, principal**).
5. We tried to (**counsel, council**) him, but it was futile.
6. A (**mantel, mantle**) of snow covered the earth.
7. A lawyer gives (**counsel, council**).
8. The desks in the classroom were (**stationary, stationery**).
9. Honesty is the (**principle, principal**) characteristic of our club.
10. The shelf above a fireplace is called a (**mantel, mantle**).

2—True-and-False Quiz

(Based on pages 15 to 23.)

Correct any statement that is false:

1. A miser is one who is **frugal.**
2. **Inveigh** means "to allure or entice."
3. To be **irresolute,** one must possess courage and act without hesitation.
4. **Astuteness** refers to wealth rather than to craft or cleverness.
5. **Principal** is never used in regard to things that can be seen with the physical eye.
6. **Despicable** may be accented on the first or second syllable.
7. **Chastisement** is pronounced like **chastity.**
8. **Secretive** has only one pronunciation.
9. **Profuse** rhymes with the verb **use.**
10. One who **mediates** is called an *arbitrator.*

3—Completion Quiz

(Based on pages 15 to 23.)

Fill each blank with a word that agrees with the thought expressed. The first syllable of the word is supplied or the definition is given at the end of the sentence.

1. One who thinks he is incapable of erring or failing is called an (infa_____) person.
2. A (com_____) room is one which is large enough to take care of our wants and necessities conveniently.
3. A speaker who jumps from one subject to another is called a (di_____) speaker.
4. I know that my mother _____ approved of my step. (silently)
5. That man can talk with _____ on almost any subject. (a four-syllable word for "ease")
6. He received a (la_____) rebuke from his employer. (belaboring; censuring severely)
7. There was an _____ discussion going on when I entered the room. (a four-syllable word meaning "lively")
8. Let us select a (vir_____) leader. (vigorous; forceful)
9. Man is an (ani_____) being.
10. I (ab_____) his boastful talk. (dislike; detest)

4—Synonym and Antonym Quiz

(Based on pages 15 to 23.)

Tell whether each word is a synonym or an antonym for the word at the left:

1. urgency — unimportance, insistence, importunity, pressure.
2. harass — tire, worry, fatigue.
3. tenable — defensible, valid, plausible, superficial.
4. profuse — prodigal, lavish, abundant, meager.
5. despicable — laudable, contemptible, paltry, sordid.
6. chastisement — discipline, honor, punishment, infliction.
7. secretive — frank, reticent, uncommunicative, reserved.
8. diffuse (*a.*) — widespread, scattered, copious, verbose, concise.
9. diffuse (*v.*) — circulate, conserve, disseminate, disperse, assemble.
10. infuse — instill, inspire, imbue, insinuate, implant.

5—Matching Quiz

(Based on pages 25 to 33.)

Have each adjective in Group I modify two nouns in Group II. Try to use each word in Group II but once.

	Group I		Group II		
1.	applicable	*a.*	argument	*p.*	person
2.	capricious	*b.*	attempt	*q.*	possibilities
3.	conciliatory	*c.*	attitude	*r.*	power
4.	credible	*d.*	capital	*s.*	reasoning
5.	credulous	*e.*	characteristics	*t.*	remarks
6.	dormant	*f.*	counsel	*u.*	rule
7.	incredible	*g.*	demand	*v.*	sermon
8.	obligatory	*h.*	discipline	*w.*	speed
9.	peremptory	*i.*	dislike	*x.*	story
10.	repugnant	*j.*	grandeur	*y.*	summons
11.	stringent	*k.*	information	*z.*	sway
12.	temporal	*l.*	letter	*aa.*	temper
13.	ungovernable	*m.*	mob	*bb.*	temperament
14.	valid	*n.*	opposition	*cc.*	visit
15.	vigorous	*o.*	order	*dd.*	wind

6—Related-Word Quiz

(Based on pages 25 to 33.)

1. What three words can you evolve from **oblige**?

2. What are the adjectival forms of **conciliate** and **prepare**?

3. Give three words related to **audible**.

4. Give two recorded sounds for the first syllable of **penalize**. What is the sound of **penal**? of **penalization**?

5. What is the noun form of: **conform**; **hospitable**?

7—Synonym and Antonym Quiz

(Based on pages 25 to 33.)

Tell whether each word at the right is a synonym or an antonym of the word at the left.

1. capricious — grave, irregular, fickle, whimsical.
2. credence — credit, belief, confidence, acceptance.
3. emolument — rebuke, loss, compensation, reward.
4. subsidize — support, assist, promote, aid.
5. temporal — eternal, transient, worldly, transitory.
6. pastoral — rural, rustic, idyllic, bucolic.
7. herculean — difficult, dangerous, powerful, debilitated.
8. conform — correspond, comply, harmonize, reconcile.
9. egotism — self-exaltation, self-praise, conceit.
10. supersede — replace, supplant, divert.

8—True-and-False Quiz

(Based on pages 25 to 33.)

Correct any statement that is wrong:

1. It is correct to give two pronunciations to **herculean**.
2. The word **egoism** means the practice of speaking or writing overmuch of oneself.
3. One might **deprecate** a suggestion by a shake of the head.
4. The antonym of **audible** is **inaudible**.
5. A **roster** is a stage for public speaking or a platform used by an orator.
6. The first syllable of **credence** is pronounced **kred**.
7. Orders which are final and imperious may be called **peremptory**.
8. A person of principle is not **repugnant** to anything that savors of fraud.
9. To **depreciate** is to lower in value.
10. The accent in **peremptory** may be on either the first or the second syllable.

9—Mixed Quiz

(Based on pages 35 to 43.)

1. How should we not use **aggravate** in formal speech?

2. Is it correct to say, "I **propose** to take care of that work next week"? If incorrect, what word would you use?

3. Try to give three words that will mean "to make angry or to embitter."

4. How does **complement** differ in meaning from **compliment**?

5. Give two adjectives and the adverb related to **extemporize**.

6. What word beginning with **ve** is given to the characteristic of violence or strong feeling?

7. Can you find the delicate distinction between **complement** and **supplement**?

8. Do you say **stay' tus** for the word **status**?

9. Is there a difference in meaning between **obstinate** and **obdurate**? Illustrate the difference if there is any.

10. What word of three syllables beginning with **clan** means "secret; concealed; underhand"?

11. Can you think of a word which means "wise; having good sense; aware"? It is a three-syllable word which begins with **sen**.

12. If a man makes a speech on the spur of the moment or has little if any preparation, he is said to do what? The word has four syllables, the first of which is **ex** and the last of which is **ize**.

13. A person is banished from society for some despicable act. What verb of three syllables, the first of which is **os**, may be used to express this idea?

14. Rewrite the following sentences, using the word in parentheses and retaining the original thought:

a. He surely deserved the reward that he received. (**merited**)

b. Let me tell you the new manager has turned this shop upside down. (**radical**)

15. What word of four syllables, the first of which is **ab** and the last **ous**, means "sparing in diet; temperate; moderate"?

10—Completion Quiz
(Based on pages 35 to 43.)

Complete the word in parentheses. The meaning where necessary is given at the end of the sentence.

1. The judge was (ob_____) in his decision that the man be sent to jail. (unyielding; three syllables, the last of which rhymes with the **ate** in **senate.**)
2. We have a (co_____) supply of paper and envelopes. (abundant; plentiful)
3. Her continual tardiness (ex_____)her employer. (to excite; to anger)
4. His (car_____) fault is stealing. (principal; chief)
5. The air was sweet and (od_____). (a three-syllable word ending in **ous**)
6. Remarks which are foolish and stupid belong to the category of (fat_____) remarks. (three syllables)
7. The class will start when its (com_____) of books arrives. (number required)
8. We may listen at almost any time of day to the works of the world's most (ill_____) musicians. (famous; eminent; great or noble)
9. He (_____posed) to put his plan into effect at the earliest opportunity.
10. We were (gal_____) by the speech. (to stimulate)

11—Mixed Quiz
(Based on pages 35 to 43.)

1. How is **puerile** pronounced?
2. Is a **fatuous** person one who is overweight?
3. Have the word **cardinal** modify two nouns.
4. Name a verb that is derived from **radical.**
5. Give another adjective related to **merited.**

12—Synonym and Antonym Quiz
(Based on pages 35 to 43.)

State whether each word at the right is a synonym or an antonym of the word at the left.

1. vehemence — forcefulness, violence, weakness, fury.
2. puerile — childish, trivial, foolish, mature.
3. obliterate — blot out, expunge, erase, retain.
4. obstinate — refractory, opinionated, intractable.
5. illustrious — renowned, distinguished, conspicuous, signal.

13—True-and-False Quiz

(Based on pages 45 to 53.)

Correct any sentences that are not true:

1. A person capable of erring is called **fallible**.
2. If prices of commodities change continually, they are said to **fluctuate**.
3. **Temerity** means shyness or diffidence.
4. It is correct to use the word **defunct** in regard to a business that is bankrupt.
5. If a boat has lost its rudder, it is said to **founder**.
6. In **amicable** the accent is placed on the second syllable.
7. **Bade** should rhyme with **glad** rather than with **aid**.
8. The word **irreparable** is correctly accented on the third syllable.
9. The second syllable of **implacable** must rhyme with **slay**.
10. **Disseminate** is a synonym for **permeate**.

14—Mixed Quiz

(Based on pages 45 to 53.)

1. Is **impregnable** related to **impregnate**?
2. What word based on **laud** means "expressing praise"?
3. Use **flounder** in regard to a speaker.
4. Can you think of three words which contain the word **vital**?
5. Write three words related to the adjective **reparable**.
6. Use in sentences: **habitual, habitat, habitation**.
7. How many syllables has **salient**? What are its noun forms?
8. Give the noun, verb, and another adjectival form of **confirmatory**.
9. Have each word modify two nouns: **vital, salient, servile, amicable**.
10. Use in sentences: **servitude, servility**.

15—Selection Quiz

(Based on pages 45 to 53.)

Select the correct word from the two words given in parentheses:

1. His speech received (**laudable, laudatory**) comment from the editors.
2. The increase of accidents (**instigated, initiated**) an investigation.
3. The rudderless ship was (**floundering, foundering**).
4. He proved to be an (**amicable, implacable**) foe.
5. The speaker (**floundered, fluctuated**) too much to be interesting.
6. He made a (**laudable, laudatory**) attempt to rescue the child.
7. A raging storm had done (**innumerable, irreparable**) damage.
8. Co-operation is (**salient, vital**) to success in the project.
9. Although he has always been accurate, he may sometime prove (**infallible, fallible**).
10. The house did not seem to be (**habituated, inhabited**).

16—Synonym and Antonym Quiz

(Based on pages 45 to 53.)

Tell whether each word at the right is a synonym or antonym of the word at the left:

1. permeate — penetrate, pervade, saturate.
2. emanate — flow, smother, radiate, issue.
3. sanction (*v.*) — validate, approve, allow, authorize, indorse.
4. corroborate — verify, confirm, substantiate, invalidate.
5. subterfuge — device, artifice, evasion, probity.

17—Association Quiz

(Based on pages 55 to 63.)

Fill the blanks in the following with the word defined at the end of the sentence. Where there is no blank, answer the question.

1. What four-syllable word would you use to convey the meaning "to restore life to; to reanimate; to reinvigorate"? One such word begins with **re** and its last syllable rhymes with **die**.
2. Can you think of a word with seven letters which begins with **rec** and means "to set right; to correct from a wrong or false state; to amend"?
3. What four words can you write that will contain the word **habit?**
4. (D_____) changes have been made in this institution within the past year. ("extreme or radical in effect"; two syllables)
5. What word with eight letters beginning with **vit** means "to endow with life; to animate"?
6. What word of four syllables ending in **ible** means "that which may be neglected or disregarded; so small or unimportant that one may disregard it"?
7. Understanding, not (eru_____), is the goal of learning. (four syllables, the last of which is **tion**)
8. He was (san_____) in the face of failure. (two syllables)
9. After a test, one should note his mistakes carefully and practice the correct form as a (rem_____) measure. (four syllables)
10. As we entered the "haunted" house, we were greeted by (har_____) cries. (heart-rending; three syllables, the last of which is **ing**)

18—Mixed Quiz

(Based on pages 55 to 63.)

1. In what respect is a **feasible** project better than a **plausible** project?

2. What is the sound of the second syllable in **remedial?**

3. Pronounce: **nefarious; poinsettia.**

4. Use in sentences the adverbial form of: **tentative; habitual.**

5. On which syllable is the accent in: **autopsy; invalidate?**

19—Selection Quiz

(*Based on pages 55 to 56.*)

Select the word in parentheses which makes the sentence correct:

1. His (**human, humane**) treatment of his help was known throughout the country.
2. Places associated with or famous in history are called (**historic, historical**).
3. If a plan can without any doubt be carried out, it is called a (**plausible, feasible**) plan.
4. It is a (**historic, historical**) fact.
5. A(n) (**valid, invalid**) excuse is an acceptable one.

20—Antonym and Synonym Quiz

(*Based on pages 55 to 63.*)

Tell whether each word at the right is an antonym or a synonym of the word at the left:

1. vivid — obscure, animated, intense, lively, brilliant.
2. interminable — endless, brief, protracted, limitless, boundless.
3. validate — substantiate, confirm, falsify.
4. nefarious — wicked, infamous, iniquitous, benevolent.
5. tentative — trial, experimental, provisional, permanent.
6. scurrilous — delicate, adulatory, abusive, coarse, indecent.
7. admirable — estimable, despicable, excellent, praiseworthy.
8. imperturbable — serene, excitable, phlegmatic, calm.
9. arbitrary — despotic, decisive, capricious, irresponsible.
10. provocative — annoying, irritating, stimulating.

21—Association Quiz

(Based on pages 65 to 73.)

1. What word of eight letters, the first syllable of which is **ex** and the last syllable of which rhymes with **sit,** means "clearly expressed; outspoken; distinctly stated; having no disguised meaning"?

2. Name a word of two syllables, the first of which is **trans** and the last of which rhymes with **sit,** which means "to send from one person or place to another; to pass along."

3. Can you think of a word of two syllables, the first letter of which is **l** and the last syllable of which rhymes with **dish,** whose meaning is "to pour out or spend profusely; to squander; to bestow with profusion"?

4. What eight-letter word beginning with **t** and ending in **ant** means "willing to let other people do as they think best; indulgent; willing to endure beliefs and actions in which one does not believe"?

5. Think of a word of two syllables that begins with **a** and rhymes with **best,** whose definition is "to bear witness to; to certify; to affirm to be true or genuine."

22—Completion Quiz

(Based on pages 65 to 73.)

Complete the word in parentheses. The meaning is given at the end of the sentence.

1. Vigorous attempts have been made to (**exter**_____ ___) the rats from this city. (to destroy completely; to root out; to annihilate)

2. Because of her (**phleg**_____) nature, she was obliged to resign from her office. (sluggish; indifferent; not easily moved)

3. The restaurant served (**delec**___ _____) meals during our vacation. (very pleasing; delightful)

4. This course in English will (**termi**_____) on the last day of the month. (to put an end to; to end; to form the conclusion of)

5. Overcoming this difficulty presented a (**red** _____) problem. (to be feared or dreaded; formidable)

23—True-and-False Quiz

(Based on pages 65 to 73.)

Correct any statement that may be incorrect:

1. The first syllable in **heinous** is pronounced **hee** to rhyme with **glee.**
2. The last syllable of **grimace** receives the accent and is pronounced to rhyme with **face.**
3. It is incorrect to place the accent on the second syllable of **desultory**: desult′ ory.
4. The accent in **explicit** should be placed on the first syllable, **ex.**
5. The first syllable of **blatant** is pronounced **blay.**

24—Mixed Quiz

(Based on pages 65 to 73.)

1. What adjective means "every two years"? "every six months"?

2. Give the correct pronunciation for **beneficent.**

3. Can you think of two words that begin with **transit?**

4. Give two synonyms for: **inscrutable; blatant.**

5. What is the verb form of **signal?**

6. Write three words that begin with **initi.**

7. Give three synonyms for **funereal.**

8. Give two words that pertain to crime or criminals which contain the syllable **crim.**

9. Place in sentences: **importunity; opportunely.**

10. Give two synonyms and two antonyms for: **desultory; inexorable.**

25—Related-Word Quiz

(Based on pages 65 to 73.)

Place each of the following related words in original sentences:

1. transmission, transmit.
2. tolerant, tolerate.
3. attest, attestation.
4. implicit, explicitly.
5. alternate, alter.

26—Completion Quiz

(Based on pages 75 to 83.)

Fill each blank with a word which will convey the necessary meaning. The definition will be found in the parentheses at the end of the sentence.

1. His remarks were only (**hy**_____) at best. (assumed without proof; supposed; concerned with hypotheses)
2. He only (**sim**_____) roughness, for at heart he was a very kind man. (to pretend; to feign; to imitate; to have the appearance of)
3. The people disliked the (**off**_____) attitude of the governor. (volunteering one's services where they are neither asked nor needed)
4. The party grew very (**hi**_____) toward midnight. (noisy; mirthful; very gay)
5. He had an (**in**_____) desire to eat. (unrestrained; four syllables)
6. The editor's (**in**_____) statement about the administration's weaknesses failed to effect any good. (sharp, penetrating, sarcastic)
7. It is hard to decide on what is the truth when reports are (**di**_____). (different; disagreeing)
8. The ideas of peace and progress seem (**com**_____). (consistent; existing harmoniously)
9. He (**ref**_____) the accusation with proof of the contrary. (to prove something false; disprove; overthrow by argument)
10. His schemes are too (**vis**_____) for anyone to put faith in them. (fanciful; fantastic; impracticable)

27—Mixed Quiz

(Based on pages 75 to 83.)

1. What is meant by **affected sympathy**?

2. Use **effect** as a verb in two different sentences.

3. Can you use **simulate** in a sentence? How does **simulate** differ in meaning from **stimulate**?

4. Give two synonyms for: **complicated; severe.**

5. Pronounce: **enigmatical; devious; impotent; accompanist.**

28—Matching Quiz

(Based on pages 75 to 83.)

Select from Group II a definition for each word in Group I:

Group I   *Group II*

Adjectives

1.	abstruse	*a.* affected	*l.*	imperious
2.	ambiguous	*b.* all-powerful	*m.*	impractical
3.	compatible	*c.* beginning	*n.*	incriminating; accusing
4.	devastating	*d.* complacent		
5.	devious	*e.* destructive	*o.*	indirect; circuitous
6.	impotent	*f.* doubtful		
7.	inordinate	*g.* excessive	*p.*	mysterious
8.	officious	*h.* extraordinary	*q.*	profound
9.	scathing	*i.* fictitious	*r.*	stupid
10.	visionary	*j.* harmonious	*s.*	wounding; injurious
		k. helpless		

Verbs

1.	coalesce	*a.* accompany	*f.*	pretend; imitate
2.	coerce	*b.* compel	*g.*	prove false
3.	justify	*c.* comply	*h.*	unite
4.	refute	*d.* distrust		
5.	simulate	*e.* give a good reason for		

29—Related-Word Quiz

(Based on pages 75 to 83.)

Use each of the following related words in a sentence. Look up the meaning of each in the dictionary to be sure that you use the word correctly.

1. scathing   — unscathed, scathe.
2. simulate   — dissimilar, dissimulate.
3. impotent   — potential, potency.
4. incisive   — decisive, concise, precise.
5. complicated   — implicate, duplicate, complicity.

30—Association Quiz

(Based on pages 85 to 93.)

1.   Can you think of a four-syllable word beginning with **re** whose last syllable rhymes with **fate,** and which means "to inflict in return; to return like for like"?

2.   Think of a four-syllable word that begins with **ad** and ends with **tion** which means "flattery or excessive praise."

3.   Give a four-syllable word beginning with **de** and ending in **ize** that means "to corrupt; to undermine the morals of; to weaken in discipline."

4.   Give a six-syllable word, beginning with **de** and ending with **tory,** meaning "threatening or condemning."

5.   Think of a three-syllable word ending in **ize** that means "to counteract; to counterbalance; to destroy the effect of."

6.   What two-syllable word beginning with **su** means "listless; indifferent to duty or the needs of others"?

7.   A confirmation or sanction may be called what five-syllable word beginning with **rati?**

8.   What three-syllable adjective beginning with **pro** is applied to a wasteful or extravagant expenditure of anything?

9.   One who talks to himself is said to do what? (a four-syllable word beginning with **s** and ending with **ize**)

10.   What three-syllable word beginning with **syn** and ending in **ize** means "to agree in time; to happen at the same time"?

31—Related-Word Quiz

(Based on pages 85 to 93.)

Use in sentences:

1.   The adjectival form of **dogmatize.**
2.   The noun form of **tyrannize.**
3.   The adverbial form of **irresistible.**
4.   The verb form of **retaliatory; derision.**
5.   Any word related to **subordinate; imputation.**

32—True-and-False Quiz

(Based on pages 85 to 93.)

Which of the following are false?

1. The verb **project** is accented on the first syllable.
2. It is now permissible to place a primary accent on the first syllable of **municipal**, thus: **mu′ nicip″ al.**
3. **Clique** may also be pronounced **click.**
4. The second syllable of **comparable** receives the accent and rhymes with **dare.**
5. To **procrastinate** is to accuse.
6. **Sedentary** has a main accent on the second syllable and a secondary accent on the last syllable.
7. **Acceptation** is the generally accepted meaning of anything.
8. **Complement** is a form of flattery or praise.
9. **Capacity** is the power to do a thing.
10. **Alloyed** happiness is unbroken, perfect happiness.

33—Synonym and Antonym Quiz

(Based on pages 85 to 93.)

Tell whether each word at the right is a synonym or an antonym of the word at the left:

1. intermittent — alternating, recurrent, continuous, periodic.
2. insidious — guileless, full of plots, crafty, deceitful, wily.
3. derision — scorn, mockery, contempt, insult, adulation.
4. inculcate — suppress, teach, instill, implant, infuse.
5. judicious — imprudent, indiscreet, sagacious, discerning.

34—Association Quiz
(Based on pages 95 to 103.)

1. Name a two-syllable word, whose first syllable is **de** and whose last syllable rhymes with **came,** which means "to injure one's reputation; to slander."

2. One who is moderate and mild in speech is said to be what? (a three-syllable adjective beginning with **tem**)

3. What word ending in **cation** means work aside from one's regular work?

4. What word ending in **lusion** is a mistaken conviction?

5. What word beginning with **vo** and ending in **ous** means "greedy or excessively eager"?

6. What four-syllable word beginning with **im** and ending in **ous** may be applied to a person who is hasty, rash, or vehement?

7. Name an adjective meaning "wealthy or abundant" and beginning in **op.**

8. What adjective beginning with **in** and ending in **id** means "dull, flat, tasteless"?

9. An inference or guess may be called what noun beginning with **conj**?

10. Give an adjective beginning with **de** and ending in **erous** that means "skillful, expert, quick."

35—Related-Word Quiz
(Based on pages 95 to 103.)

1. Give the noun form of: **deride; callous; opprobrious.**

2. Give two noun forms of **fraudulent.**

3. What is the verb form of **dogmatic?**

4. Give a four-syllable noun related to **predatory.**

5. Give the adjective meaning "of strong opinions."

6. Give three nouns related to **mandatory.**

7. Give two nouns related to **diversify.**

8. Name four words containing the word **diction.**

9. How many words do you know that are related to **somnolent?** Write three.

10. Name four words related to **contributory.**

36—True-and-False Quiz

(Based on pages 95 to 103.)

Correct any statement that may be false:

1. There is no such word in the English language as **ekzee′ ma**. The word **eczema** must be accented on the first syllable: **ek′ zema**.
2. The first syllable in **zoology** is pronounced **zoo** to rhyme with glue: **zoo ol′ ogy**.
3. In the hyphenated word **long-lived** the last part is pronounced to rhyme with **thrived**.
4. A **mirage** is an **allusion**.
5. A **majority** is more than half the whole number.
6. **Benefaction** means good will or kindly feeling.
7. The first syllable of **truculent** rhymes with **struck**.
8. **Somnolent** is accented on the second syllable.
9. **Gardenia** is pronounced **gar din′ i a**.
10. It is incorrect to give the third syllable of **associate** the sound of **sh**.
11. The medical term for lockjaw is accented on the middle syllable: **tetan′ us**.
12. The final **t** of **robot** is not sounded.
13. The word **quintuplets** is accented on the first syllable only.
14. **Communiqué** is accented on the next to the last syllable.
15. The only pronunciation for the third syllable of **appreciative** is **shi**.

37—Completion Quiz

(Based on pages 105 to 113.)

Complete the word in parentheses to make the sentence meaningful. The exact meaning of the word wanted appears at the end of the sentence.

1. With his consistently high marks, Peter had achieved a very (envi_____) record. (fit to excite envy)
2. Behind his miserliness is his fear of (pen_____). (want)
3. A (sub_____) nature prevented his success as a leader. (obedient)
4. Colorful descriptions and the inclusion of important details make up the (gr_____) accounts of the big games. (vivid, picturesque)
5. He pleaded that he was not (cul_____) of any of the charges made against him. (blameworthy)
6. The least irritation brings out his (bel_____) tendencies. (contentious; pugnacious)
7. Some (sed_____) writers steadily produce a novel each year for as many as forty years without intermission. (industrious)
8. (Sed_____) attacks upon the government are likely to secure one a jail sentence. (exciting resistance to authority)
9. The distinguished gathering suddenly discovered itself in a very (ris_____) situation. (laugh-provoking)
10. It is habitual for him to (cal_____) anyone whom he finds in his way. (accuse falsely of crimes or offenses)

38—Synonym and Antonym Quiz

(Based on pages 105 to 113.)

Tell whether each word at the right is a synonym or an antonym of the word at the left:

1. ponderous — oppressive, spirited, labored, dull, weighty
2. pungent — caustic, penetrating, stinging, vapid.
3. coercion — force, compulsion, constraint, toleration.
4. symbolize — typify, represent, express, designate.
5. delusive — trustworthy, deceptive, false, beguiling.

39—Related-Word Quiz
(Based on pages 105 to 113.)

1. Use in sentences two adjectives related to **envy**.

2. Which word would you use to convey the meaning "to rise from; to come out into view," **emerge** or **immerge**?

3. Can you think of four words in which is found the syllable **merge**?

4. Use **respective** and **respectable** in sentences.

5. Give the adjectival form of **demonstrate**.

6. Give two adjectival forms of **appreciate**.

7. Give two words beginning with **belli** which refer to fighting.

8. How many words can you give containing the syllable **ris**?

9. Write three words that are related to **delusion**.

10. How many words related to **defection** do you know?

40—Selection Quiz
(Based on pages 105 to 113.)

Select the word in parentheses that makes the sentence correct:

1. We are gradually (**immerging, emerging**) from the depression.
2. He thought that he could (**elude, delude**) us into believing the scheme a worthy cause.
3. Seats at the banquet were assigned according to the (**respective, respectable**) ranks of the guests.
4. They are gradually (**immerging, emerging**) into seclusion.
5. What did you (**induce, deduce**) from his lecture?

41—Completion Quiz

(Based on pages 115 to 123.)

Complete the word in parentheses to make the sentence correct. The meaning is given at the end of the sentence.

1. We made many attempts to (**ingr**————————) ourselves with our superiors. (to bring into favor)
2. Brown received a (**sin**————————) for his political work. (office of value with little responsibility)
3. Capitalism and labor has always been a (**cont**————————) question. (quarrelsome; characterized by heated argument)
4. One should strive to develop a (**ten**————————) memory. (holding fast; capable of retaining)
5. There was no need of his assuming such a (**super**————————) attitude toward his employees. (haughty, disdainful, contemptuous)
6. Do you not believe in the (**eff**————————) of prayer? (power to produce desired results)
7. Clerks dislike to wait upon her because she is so extremely (**fas**————————). (hard to please; dainty in taste; overnice)
8. A speech that tends to excite anger or animosity is called an (**infl**————————) speech.
9. When he realized the inconvenience that his (**dil**————————) conduct had caused, Jones determined to be ever after prompt and on the alert. (tending to delay; characterized by slowness; tardy)
10. He will regret that he (**rep**————————) his friends' offers of help. (to refuse to accept; to cast off)

42—Antonym and Synonym Quiz

(Based on pages 115 to 123.)

Tell whether each word at the right is a synonym or an antonym of the word at the left:

1. invidious — offensive, unenviable, hateful.
2. factious — agreeable, amiable, seditious, dissentious, contentious.
3. pretentious — ostentatious, affected, pompous, unassuming.
4. infectious — communicable, contaminating, sanitary.
5. enervate — weaken, enfeeble, debilitate, invigorate, unnerve.
6. expert (*adj.*) — adroit, awkward, dexterous, proficient.
7. gratis — gratuitously, onerously, bountifully.
8. transcendent — superior, surpassing, ordinary.
9. inconceivable — unthinkable, incredible, obvious.
10. senile — aged, infirm, juvenile.

43—Selection Quiz

(*Based on pages 115 to 123.*)

Select the correct word in parentheses:

1. The small amount of charitable work done by the millionaire proved that he was a(n) (**penurious, impecunious**) person.
2. One could not help being charmed with her (**complacent, complaisant**) manner.
3. He had not believed that he would (**assimilate, simulate**) so many facts in so short a time.
4. He is a (**complacent, complaisant**) old wretch as utterly devoted to himself as a hermit.
5. The companions of his youth were gone, and he now lived in a garret, old, (**penurious, impecunious**), and alone.

44—Pronunciation Quiz

(*Based on pages 115 to 123.*)

1. What choice have you for the pronunciation of **gratis**?

2. What is the sound of the last syllable in **column**?

3. On what syllable should you accent **enervate**?

4. What choice have you for pronouncing **expert**, the adjective?

5. Can you give a word rhyming with **corps**?

6. Is it incorrect to pronounce **apparatus: apparay' tus**?

7. Pronounce **alias**. Check both accent and sound.

8. What is the American pronunciation of **decade**?

9. May we pronounce **root** like the word **foot**?

10. What sound has the **s** in **complaisant**?

45—Quiz
(*Based on pages 125 to 133.*)

1. If you wish to express the thought "to clothe with authority or legal power," what three-syllable word beginning with **au** and ending in **ize** would you use?

2. Suppose that you wish to reduce a mistake to the smallest degree possible. What word of three syllables, the first of which is **min**, would express your thought?

3. You refuse to be seen in the company of a certain person, for so doing may endanger your position. What verb of three syllables, the first of which is **jeop**, may be used to express this thought?

4. "The ideal person is able to make his own sunshine or happiness." What word of three syllables, the first of which is **gen**, could be used figuratively in this sentence?

5. "What prevented you from seeing the governor yesterday?" What word of two syllables which begins with **de** and rhymes with **her** may be used in this sentence?

6. When a lawyer is expelled from the legal profession, which prefix is used with **bar** to explain the case, **de** or **dis**?

7. Why do you think **urbane** has come to mean "refined or polite"?

8. Would you call a swollen stream **turgid** or **turbid**?

9. Can you think of three words each of which begins with **urb**?

10. His friends condoled with him on his (lam_____) failure to win the match. (pitiable, deplorable, mournful)

46—Synonym and Antonym Quiz
(*Based on pages 125 to 133.*)

Tell whether each word at the right is a synonym or an antonym of the word at the left:

1. **ebullition** — agitation, outburst, quiescence, effervescence, commotion.
2. **assumption** — appropriation, usurpation, arrogance, humility.
3. **constrain** — tolerate, compel, necessitate, repress.
4. **debility** — fortitude, languor, feebleness.
5. **contrite** — penitent, obdurate, humble, sorrowful.

47—Completion Quiz

(*Based on pages 125 to 133.*)

Adjectives		Verbs	
abortive	mundane	authorize	invigorate
capacious	potent	debar	jeopardize
capricious	potential	disbar	minimize
circuitous	recondite	disintegrate	rejuvenate
cumbrous	turbid	generate	signalize
impotent	turgid		
incongruous	urban		
momentous	urbane		

Fill each blank with the correct word from the list:

1. You will find the latest model of our deluxe coupé even more _____ than last year's model.
2. The _____ route over the mountain took several hours longer than we expected.
3. He cannot be forthright, but must use long and _____ ways to express himself.
4. Release from the burden of unhappiness had practically _____ him.
5. Nothing will so _____ you as an early-morning dip in the cool, exhilarating surf.
6. Soon the organization will not exist, because it is fast _____.
7. Her enthralling voice makes her a(n) _____ prima donna.
8. His tales were too _____ to be believed.
9. A lawyer whose license to practice law has been revoked is said to have been _____.
10. The _____ waters of the flood inundated many cities.
11. Rural and _____ customs are not always the same.
12. His kind and _____ disposition won for him many friends.
13. The stream was too _____ for us to see bottom.
14. His infirmity _____ him from participating in football.
15. He is one of the most _____ mayors this city has ever had; he has accomplished more in one administration than most mayors do in two or three.
16. His use of _____ words and expressions detracts from his style.
17. The rebels made a(n) _____ attempt to assassinate the king.
18. Who _____ you to purchase those cars?
19. The newspapers endeavored to _____ the results of the rioting.
20. You will _____ your health if you attempt to make the trip in this weather.

48—Mixed Quiz
(Based on pages 135 to 143.)

1. Would you say that **ingenious** is in any way related to the word **genius**?

2. What is the meaning of **disingenuous**?

3. If **ingenuous** means "frank; candid; free from disguise," what is the meaning of **ingenuity**?

4. How does **continuous** differ from **continual**?

5. When a person examines a report very closely to be certain that it contains no mistake, he is said to _____ the report. The word required has three syllables, the first of which is **scru**. What is it?

6. An effective way to learn to spell is to endeavor to see the word with the mental eye. What verb of four syllables, the first of which is **vis**, will express this idea?

7. Is a person who is clever, talented, or skillful **ingenuous** or **ingenious**?

49—Completion Quiz
(Based on pages 135 to 143.)

Complete the word in parentheses so that the sentence will be correct. The meaning of the desired word appears at the end of the sentence.

1. He was rebuked for his (**except**_____) remarks. (objectionable)
2. Her (**ingen**_____) confession elicited sympathy from the judge. (free from disguise)
3. The New Deal was derided by some and (**eul**_____) by others. (to praise; to write or speak in praise of)
4. This work must be done as (**exped**_____) as possible. (speedily)
5. He has an (**except**_____) command of the English language. (better than the average)
6. His talk was too (**rep**_____) to be entertaining. (full of repetitions; repeating)
7. The goods were obtained in a (**sur**_____) way. (stealthy; secret; done without authority)
8. His (**os**_____) aim was to help his friends. ("apparent"; four syllables)
9. The prosecuting attorney was (**rel**_____) in his drive upon criminals. ("stern or persistent"; three syllables)
10. The (**pred**_____) note of his speech was charity. (prevailing)

50—Completion Quiz

(Based on pages 135 to 143.)

Verbs		Adjectives	
amplify	archaic	onerous	salient
eulogize	cautious	ostensible	sepulchral
incapacitate	disputatious	practicable	surreptitious
scrutinize	inherent	practical	timorous
visualize	obsolescent	predominant	vapid
	obsolete	relentless	venomous

Fill each blank with the word from the list which fits the sense most accurately:

1. The main part of the speech was devoted to ＿＿＿＿＿ the details and scope of the plan.
2. He was ＿＿＿＿＿ in his desire to overcome his competitor.
3. To him, study is a(n) ＿＿＿＿＿ duty.
4. His movements about the place were as ＿＿＿＿＿ as a cat's.
5. To picture in the mind is to ＿＿＿＿＿.
6. The lack of the power of forceful, smooth speech ＿＿＿＿＿ him whenever he was asked to address a group.
7. The old man's voice was weird and ＿＿＿＿＿.
8. He is inclined to the visionary rather than to the ＿＿＿＿＿.
9. This type of architecture one must search far to find; it is almost ＿＿＿＿＿.
10. It seems that the most adverse circumstances cannot destroy his ＿＿＿＿＿ good nature.
11. It is an interesting plan, but probably is not ＿＿＿＿＿.
12. Although the ＿＿＿＿＿ purpose of this plan is to stimulate commerce, we suspect that it is really only a political move.
13. He is ＿＿＿＿＿, and will take no risk without first investigating every possible source of danger.
14. ＿＿＿＿＿ words are not likely to be understood, and ＿＿＿＿＿ words are not in the best taste, since they are being superseded by newer ones.
15. His ＿＿＿＿＿ attacks upon the new manager cost him his job.

51—Selection Quiz

(Based on pages 145 to 153.)

Select the word in parentheses which conveys the correct sense of the sentence:

1. Because of his low scholastic marks, he was declared (**illegible, ineligible**) to play football.
2. (**Aphasia, amnesia**) sufferers usually have other attendant ills which keep them at home or in a hospital, while (**aphasia, amnesia**) victims are frequently found wandering about the streets.
3. The society is trying to obtain the (**exemption, extirpation**) of gambling in the town.
4. A (**vernal, whimsical**) freshness about the little old lady's sparkling face and pleasant manner evoked thoughts of the exuberance of spring or youth rather than of the pains of age.
5. The lecturer covers much ground in an hour, for he habitually speaks in a (**garrulous, succinct**) manner.

52—Synonym and Antonym Quiz

(Based on pages 145 to 153.)

State whether the words at the right are antonyms or synonyms of the word at the left:

1. dilapidated   — neglected, misused, preserved, decayed.
2. abeyance   — suspension, suppression, extension.
3. impeach   — accuse, eulogize, discredit, arraign.
4. abominable   — detestable, loathsome, pleasing.
5. cadaverous   — ghastly, haggard, robust, gaunt.
6. appreciable   — estimable, distinguishable, perceptible, imperceptible.
7. paramount   — pre-eminent, distinguished, superior, surpassing.
8. accrue   — augment, result, accumulate, diminish.
9. mitigate   — soften, moderate, appease, augment.
10. allay   — relieve, quell, calm, repress, aggravate.

53—Mixed Quiz

(Based on pages 145 to 153.)

1. Give the definition of each of these words: **illegal**; **ineligible**; **illegible**.

2. What name do you give to writing that is incapable of being read?

3. What does **amnesia** mean?

4. Give three synonyms for **allay** (beginning with: **al, as,** and **mit**).

5. What sound has the **a** in **digitalis**? In **garrulous**?

6. How many syllables has **maestro**? What is the sound of the **a** in this word?

7. How many accents are there in **remuneration,** and where do they fall?

8. How many syllables has **abominable**? Do you sound them all?

9. What sound has the second syllable of **abeyance**?

10. Give the sound of the last syllable in **succinct**.

54—Matching Quiz

(Based on pages 145 to 153.)

Find a definition in Column II for each word in Column I:

I		II	
		a.	amenable
		b.	concise
		c.	delicate; frail
1.	diffuse	*d.*	educational
2.	fragile	*e.*	fanciful; odd
3.	furtive	*f.*	incapable of being read
4.	illegible	*g.*	not legal
5.	ineligible	*h.*	not qualified
6.	rhetorical	*i.*	obstinate
7.	satirical	*j.*	oratorical
8.	succinct	*k.*	sarcastic
9.	tractable	*l.*	severe in ridiculing
10.	whimsical	*m.*	stealthy
		n.	unrestrained; widespread
		o.	unsuccessful

55—Matching Quiz

(Based on pages 155 to 163.)

Find in Column II a definition for each word in Column I:

I   II

Verbs

                    a. to agitate
                    b. to be diffused throughout

1. contemptible   *c.* to carry; to enrapture
2. contemptuous   *d.* to change in appearance or character
3. efface   *e.* to discourse; to speak at length
4. expansive   *f.* to erase
5. fluster   *g.* to light up
6. frustrate   *h.* to make clear; to explain
7. illumine   *i.* to prevent from attaining a purpose
8. immoderate   *j.* to withdraw or renounce
9. impalpable
10. ineffable   *Adjectives*
11. inevitable
12. pervade   *k.* able to spread
13. recant   *l.* deserving of scorn
14. transform   *m.* incapable of being tempted
15. transport   *n.* inexpressible
                    o. intolerable; insupportable
                    p. scornful
                    q. sure to happen
                    r. that which cannot be felt
                    s. unreasonable

56—Mixed Quiz

(Based on pages 155 to 163.)

1. If you called an honest man a thief, would that be a **contemptible** or a **contemptuous** remark, or both?

2. If a speaker appeared confused or muddled on being introduced, would you say that he was **frustrated** or **flustered**?

3. To go beyond the limits of something is described by what verb beginning with **trans**?

4. Give an adjective meaning "not doubtful" closely related to the word **doubt**.

5. Give a synonym for: **voluble**; **fictitious**.

6. Name three words related to **illumine**.

7. What is the present meaning of **fabricate**? The original meaning?

8. Have each adjective modify two nouns: **legitimate**; **detestable**; **perfunctory**.

9. Where is the accent placed in the noun **transport**?

10. Write two words related to each of the following: **cognizant**; **irrevocably**; **pervade**.

57—Completion Quiz

(Based on pages 155 to 163.)

Complete the word in parentheses to make the sentence correct. The definition of the word required is given at the end of the sentence.

1. You will wish you might (**ret**_____) your angry words. (to recover)

2. A (**stri**_____) voice is one that is high-pitched or harsh-sounding. (shrill)

3. Edison had a marvellously (**prol**_____) mind. (highly inventive; productive)

4. (**Ex**_____) grounds surround the house. ("extensive"; three syllables)

5. These three (**vol**_____) speakers demanded the floor at once. (of ready or rapid speech)

58—Mixed Quiz
(Based on pages 165 to 173.)

1. What is the meaning of **recalcitrant**?

2. What word beginning with **s** and ending with **brious** means "favorable to health, beneficial"?

3. What is the noun form of **solemnize**?

4. Which of the two words **sensuous** and **sensual** is now used in a favorable or neutral sense?

5. What is the adjective related to **elucidate**?

6. Have each adverb modify two adjectives: **unquestionably; strenuously; rigidly.**

7. How do you pronounce: **modify; salutary**?

8. On which syllable of **obsess** is the accent placed?

9. How should you sound the first **e** of **elucidate**?

10. What is the sound of the **u** in: **inured; spurious**?

59—Synonym and Antonym Quiz
(Based on pages 165 to 173.)

State whether each word at the right is a synonym or an antonym of the word at the left:

1. tangible — impalpable, perceptible, substantial, evident.
2. obsess — beset, harass, engross, relieve.
3. acrimonious — pungent, mordant, caustic, acrid.
4. spurious — sham, genuine, counterfeit.
5. circumvent — frustrate, encompass, delude.

60—Completion Quiz

(Based on pages 165 to 173.)

Verbs		Adjectives	
beguile	humanize	callous	pertinacious
capitalize	illuminate	circumspect	rigorous
capitulate	liberalize	circumstantial	salubrious
consecrate	modify	imperative	salutary
dominate	necessitate	intangible	sensual
elucidate	solemnize	inured	sensuous
		lugubrious	tangible

Fill each blank in the following sentences with the correct word from the above lists:

1. A climate favorable to one's health is called a _____ climate.
2. To build another high school will _____ an extra tax.
3. The talk had a(n) _____ effect upon the young man.
4. Few successful businesses are started without some _____ assets.
5. The Tomb of the Unknown Soldier is _____ to our unknown World War dead.
6. We asked the teacher to _____ the electron theory.
7. We soon became _____ to such petty disturbances, and they ceased to irritate us.
8. The young man has decided to _____ on his tennis ability.
9. We do not wish to _____ our criminal laws.
10. The work is _____; it cannot be neglected.
11. The _____ winters of northern regions develop physical stamina.
12. The day and minute of the signing of the Armistice have been annually _____.
13. His pleasures were not all _____: some that gave him the most gratification were mental or intellectual.
14. It is unthinkable that so _____ a driver could be involved in so serious an accident.
15. Whipping and other forms of corporal punishment disappeared in the attempt to _____ education.
16. While _____ evidence would indicate that international affairs are at a standstill, war may be brewing.
17. The younger boys dropped their persecution of him when they found him _____ to their ridicule.
18. He finds a(n) _____ charm in all the seasons.
19. The vocational adviser asked the student whether he found it more natural to _____ or to carry out the plans of others.
20. The setting of the opening of *Il Penseroso* is designed to develop a _____ mood.

61—Completion Quiz

(Based on pages 175 to 183.)

adroit	fragmentary	impunity
aver	frantic	inveterate
averse	healthful	paucity
avert	healthy	recoil
elusive	idiotic	spontaneity
estrange	illusive	valorous

Fill each blank in the following sentences with the correct word from the above list:

1. He _____ that he was not guilty.
2. *Aversion* bears a relationship in meaning to _____.
3. He is a _____ child.
4. The mountain air proved very _____.
5. The boy's parents were _____ to his playing football.
6. No attempt was made to _____ the financial disaster.
7. He is noted for his _____ use of words.
8. He put off our inquiries with such _____ answers that we were able to learn nothing about the situation.
9. His pertinacious insistence upon having his own way _____ his family from him.
10. One should not feel when traveling abroad that as a foreign citizen he can break the laws of a country with _____.
11. Mirror-lined walls gave the room a(n) _____ appearance of width.
12. The people of some southern countries are renowned for the _____ of their artistic ability.
13. While we _____ from thoughts of warfare, we will not willingly submit to an aggressor.
14. The teacher advocated a steady study pace rather than a(n) _____ attempt to memorize one's notes the day before an examination.
15. His knowledge of the main events of the Restoration period was too _____ to allow him to pass the test in English History.

62—Mixed Quiz

(Based on pages 175 to 183.)

1.   If a man lives in a very comfortable and palatial house, with what four-syllable word beginning with **lu** and ending in **ious** would you describe it?

2.   Can you think of a five-syllable adjective that begins with **par**, meaning "stingy; frugal to excess; sparing in expenditure of money"?   The last syllable is **ous**.

3.   Define **aver** and **avert**.

4.   Can a climate or place be **healthy**?   Explain your answer.

5.   What is the word meaning "to precede in time; to date as of a time prior to execution"?

6.   What name is given to a remedy to counteract a poison?

7.   What is the adjective beginning with **ant** that means "prior; going before"?

8.   Use in a sentence the noun form of **frantic**.

9.   Can you give one word meaning "opposed to society or the principles on which it is based"?

10.   Use in a sentence the adjective form of **spontaneity**.

11.   Use in a sentence the adjective **punitive**.

12.   What word beginning with **ob** and ending in **ious** means "forgetful; not conscious of"?

13.   Use in a sentence the noun form of **depraved**.

14.   How are the words **obvious** and **obviate** related? (Consult your dictionary.)

15.   Can you give a word beginning with **punc** and ending in **ious** that means "exact in details; very careful"?

63—Association Quiz

(Based on pages 185 to 193.)

Fill the blanks in the following sentences with the word that makes the sentence correct. The desired word is defined at the end of the sentence.

1. One should strive to (**subju**_____) pleasure to work. (to subdue; to make subservient; to bring under the yoke of power or government)
2. Some teachers still use the methods of instruction that were in vogue fifty years ago. These teachers should conform with the present-day method of instructing pupils. What should they do to their teaching? The word has three syllables, the first of which is **mod** and the last of which is **ize.**
3. The work will be (**consum**_____) before we return to school. (to complete; to finish; to fulfill; to raise to the highest point or degree)
4. He was (**dep**_____) to make our apologies for our absence at the dinner. (to empower to act in behalf of)
5. There are no (**omni**_____) persons on earth. (able in every respect and for every work)
6. It seems that public opinion against the executive is beginning to (**crys**_____). (to assume a fixed and definite form)
7. "I (**adv**_____) the measure because I believed it would be generally beneficial to both business and industrial groups," the Senator explained. (to recommend publicly; to support)
8. His (**cred**_____) of any well-presented argument kept him in a dilemma. (belief or readiness of belief)
9. The (**inhi**_____) placed upon them failed to keep the students from smoking. (restraint; act of prohibiting)
10. Every year we read of attempts to (**res**_____) the hulls of unfortunate ships or any remaining contents of ancient pirate vessels from the bottom of the sea. (to bring to view that which was forgotten or lost)
11. The more we learn, the more convinced we become that it is impossible for anyone to become (**omni**_____). (having universal knowledge; knowing all things)
12. The croaking of frogs and answering peepers, the hoot of a discontented owl, the periodical lugubrious notes of a whippoorwill's monotonous song, and other (**noc**_____) sounds unfamiliar to him contrived to keep him half awake most of the night at camp. (occurring in the night; moving about at night)
13. Psychologists have found decreasing periods of practice, at decreasing intervals, starting immediately following learning, to be the most (**exp**_____) means of permanent learning. (practical and efficient; advantageous)

14. The fact that he had so recently (**frat**⎯⎯⎯⎯⎯) with the culprit involved him in the act, to most people's thinking. (to associate in a brotherly way; to be friendly)
15. To do one's work thoroughly can be (**discred**⎯⎯⎯⎯) to no one. (injurious to reputation; disgraceful)

64—Matching Quiz

(Based on pages 185 to 193.)

Find in the column at the right the definition of each word at the left:

Adjectives

a. carried to the utmost degree
b. distrustful of one's powers
c. enshrined; personified
d. free from fault or error

1. assail
2. complicity
3. consummate (*a.*)
4. consummate (*v.*)
5. credible
6. creditable
7. diffident
8. expunge
9. impeccable
10. incarnate
11. incredulous
12. inexplicable
13. malleable
14. orgy
15. petulant

e. incapable of being explained
f. not apt to believe on slight evidence
g. quick to take offense; irritable
h. small, unimportant
i. that can be shaped; adaptable
j. worthy of belief
k. worthy of judicious praise

Nouns

l. excessive indulgence; drunken revelry
m. large number; multitude
n. participation in wrongdoing

Verbs

o. to achieve; to fulfill
p. to acquit; to absolve
q. to assault; to attack violently
r. to strike out; to destroy

65—Mixed Quiz

(Based on pages 185 to 193.)

1. Give the noun form of **expedient**. Does **expedient** always mean "best according to the moral law"?

2. On which syllable is **incarnate** accented?

3. Where is the primary accent in **omnipresent** placed?

4 Where is the accent placed in **omnivorous**?

5. May **inexplicable** ever be pronounced **in eks plik′ able**?

66—Dictionary Quiz

(Based on pages 195 to 203.)

1. "The mistake was scarcely noticeable." What word of four syllables, the first of which is **per,** could be used to express the idea of "noticeable"?

2. When an army sees almost certain defeat ahead, the leader is ready to surrender on certain conditions. What word of four syllables, the first of which is **ca** and the last of which rhymes with **gate,** means "to surrender on certain terms"?

3. If a man spends time at golf to the detriment of his business and home, he is said to make a sort of god of this sport. What word of two syllables, the first of which is **fe,** could be used to express his devotion to the game?

4. Can you think of a word of two syllables, the first of which is **cap,** that means "the heading of a chapter, section, page, or article"?

5. "If two large industries become as one, they are said to _____." What one-syllable word beginning with **f** or with **m** may be used here?

6. "When a person will not take back an uttered statement, he is said to refuse to _____ what he said." What word of two syllables, the last of which rhymes with **act,** may be used in the blank?

7. "What the speaker said was _____ to three things." What four-syllable word beginning with **re** and ending in **ible,** meaning "capable of being reduced, or of being changed to another form" could be used here?

8. "The road was not _____ because of the rains." What is the missing word? It begins with **ac** and ends in **ible,** and is defined "easy to reach; approachable."

9. "There was an attempt to form a _____ party." What word of four syllables, the last of which is **tion,** meaning "a combination or union; an alliance," is missing?

10. "He has sent me a _____ for more supplies." What four-syllable word beginning with **re** and ending in **tion,** which means "a formal written demand," is lacking?

67—Selection Quiz

(Based on pages 195 to 203.)

If one of the two words given defines the word in bold type, draw a circle around its number. Otherwise, place an **X** in the blank at the right.

Check your results with the dictionary.

1. The remarks were **caustic**.   1. sarcastic   2. terse   _____
2. The parties **fused**.   1. quarreled   2. separated   _____
3. A storm was **imminent**.   1. threatening   2. forecasting   _____
4. Popular feeling **prophesied** a change.   1. suspended   2. impended   _____
5. His attitude is **comprehensible**.   1. misunderstood   2. unreasonable   _____
6. His career **culminated** in this success.   1. ended   2. began   _____
7. He has a **dynamic** personality.   1. energetic   2. contentious   _____
8. He will be **remunerated** for his work.   1. praised   2. paid   _____
9. The judgment required a **rendition** of the goods.   1. surrender   2. destruction   _____
10. We **emulate** their splendid example.   1. imitate   2. admire   _____

68—Matching Quiz

(Based on pages 195 to 203.)

Find in the column at the right the definition of each word at the left:

1.	alienable	*a.*	capable of being destroyed
2.	captious	*b.*	capable of diffusing or instilling
3.	destructible	*c.*	capable of transformation or conversion
4.	inadmissible	*d.*	fascinating; enchanting
5.	inimitable	*e.*	fault-finding; eager to object
6.	transfusable	*f.*	harrowing; heart-rending
7.	translucent	*g.*	incessant; persevering
8.	transmutable	*h.*	matchless; beyond imitation
9.	unpredictable	*i.*	not proper to be allowed or received
10.	unremitting	*j.*	shining or glowing through; partly transparent
		k.	that can be taken away
		l.	that cannot be foreseen
		m.	that which may be held fixed or motionless

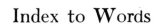

Index to Words

Index to Words

273